Prophetess of our Time

*Conversations with
Father Benedict Groeschel
and Monsignor John Esseff*

Linda Schaefer

Published by Linda Schaefer
P.O. Box 1346 Ada, Oklahoma 74821
(580) 235-5674

Cover design and composition: Michael Pounds
Interior design and layout: Michael Pounds
Editors: Cherie Peters, Fred Miller, George Snyder
Proofing: Rosemarie Benya

For orders other than individuals, Linda Schaefer grants discounts on purchases of 10 or more copies of single titles. Schaefer's book *Come and See: A Photojournalist's Journey into the World of Mother Teresa* is available for charitable causes.

ISBN-978-0-615-80711-9

Photographs © Linda Schaefer
Contributing photography: Monsignor John Esseff, Joan Habib, Sally Martin, Father Michael Van der Peet
Copyright © 2013 by Linda Schaefer

http://www.motherteresaofcalcutta.com

Dedication:

Prophetess of Our Time *is dedicated to Mother Teresa who brought so much more into my life. I would like to thank the countless people who made this book possible: Monsignor John Esseff, Father Benedict Groeschel and Sister Tarcisia, for their gift of the stories behind the book.*

I am grateful to Cherie Peters, George Snyder and Fred Miller for their diligent editing skills. I pay special tribute to my student Michael Pounds who spent many months assembling the words and photographs into these photo essays about Mother Teresa's life.

Lastly, I would like to thank an anonymous benefactor who keeps giving and believing in me enough to fly me around the world on these searches and journeys of faith.

Contents

Foreword by Cherie Peters

Cherie and her husband Paul

I own a Catholic bookstore in a suburb of Atlanta, and one day I received a call from a woman who said she was a photojournalist. She had compiled photographs of Mother Teresa and merged them into a calendar. She asked if she could spend an afternoon at my store autographing and selling them. I thought this was a great idea, and we had a delightful afternoon chatting as she shared fascinating stories about her encounters with Mother Teresa and Pope John Paul II.

I was raised Presbyterian, but married a Catholic, and when I married, I promised to raise my children Catholic. I eventually joined the Catholic Church when I was 30 years old, even though I truly didn't believe many of the teachings of the Catholic faith. I felt the Pope and the Church were old-fashioned and behind the times in the birth control debate, but firmly believed in the doctrine of the Eucharist and that abortion was a grave, moral sin. I had always admired Mother Teresa and felt that since she was Catholic, the Church couldn't be too bad! After a long journey of studying the history and reasons behind all the Church's controversial teachings, I became a staunch defender and apologist for the Catholic faith, and opened a Catholic bookstore. I even took the name Teresa for my confirmation name, even though she was still alive at the time.

After Linda's first book was published, she came several times to the store for book signings and we were able to continue our spirited discussions about God, the New Age, the Catholic Church, politics and other religions. Linda has a uniquely special place in my heart, as I have seldom met a kinder, more caring, more compassionate free spirit. Her tender concern for the poor and homeless, the destitute and underprivileged, resonated with my passionate desire to end corruption and abuse. Linda's selfless courage and conviction are a shining light in a world darkened by selfishness, materialism and greed.

I felt a kindred spirit with Linda, since my spiritual journey sometimes paralleled her own unorthodox search, and I had explored psychics Ruth Montgomery and Edgar Cayce, the New Age, reincarnation and seances, before jumping full throttle into Catholicism. It has been a pleasure to witness her spiritual journey grow from interest in the new age, to Christianity in the Catholic Church.

I was both thrilled and stunned when Linda called me after she had attended Mother Teresa's beatification and announced she was joining the Catholic Church. During her trip to Rome, she heard Mother Teresa inviting her to join the Catholic Church, and even though Linda didn't have all the answers in her quest, she was going to take a leap in faith.

Our relationship has always been based on mutual respect for each other's beliefs, even though at times those beliefs were quite different. Since the first time we spoke, I knew God was calling her to be Catholic; I also knew she had to find her way to God in her own place and time.

Introduction

Sister Laura Combona and Sister Agnes enjoy their Christmas gift, my book **Come and See**

Prophetess of Our Time begins with my 2003 journey to Rome, Italy for the beatification of Mother Teresa and closes with another journey I took to Rome with my son over Christmas in 2012. On this Christmas Day I stared into the expansive white arms of St. Peter's Square and have a conversation with two nuns I met that morning on Via della Conciliazione before Christmas Mass at Santa Maria Transpontina Church. The church is located on the same street that connects St. Peter's to the Castel Sant' Angelo on the banks of the Tiber River. I'm sure many auspicious conversations have occurred in these holy places of communion.

My greatest opportunities as a photo-journalist have almost always begun with a conversation; while these dialogues serve as the source of this second book, I have decided to include two main conversations herein. They are taped meetings with Father Benedict Groeschel and Monsignor John Esseff.

After completing my first book about my Mother Teresa, **Come and See**, I attended her beatification in Rome by Pope John Paul II. At the time I believed my work with Mother Teresa was over and that my life would go back to normal; pursuing freelance work to support my son and myself. Instead, on the 2003 Alitalia return flight back to the United States, I was urged by another passenger who went by the name, "Mr. Hugo," to have a conversation with another fellow traveler, Father James McCurry, who I was told had given dozens of retreats for Mother Teresa.

Mr. Hugo, a rotund and gregarious New Yorker, told me that over the years he had provided the thousands of tin miraculous medals Mother Teresa presented to volunteers and visitors arriving at the Mother House in Kolkata. He also told me that as a wealthy retired man, he spent much of his time driving the sisters around New York in his Lexus.

Hugo's generosity apparently included paying for the transportation of a number of clerics to Rome for the beatification of his beloved Mother Teresa. One recipient of his kind-

Castel Sant' Angelo Rome, Italy

ness was Father James McCurry of Maryland, a Marian Franciscan priest from the order of the Grey Friars of Great Britain and Ireland.

Even though I was suffering from an extreme case of bronchitis, I continued my conversation with Hugo, and at his insistence was introduced to Father James, seated a few aisles behind me. Before long, I was pulling out my small Canon video camera and recording our conversation in-between frequent bouts of coughing. By the end of the trip, I had made plans with Father James to visit him at the monastery in Ellicott, Maryland where he then resided.

It was on this flight back to Atlanta that I realized that God was calling me to continue my mission to share my encounters with Mother Teresa with the world. I had no idea how it would evolve over the next ten years, but thanks to the generous support of an anonymous benefactor from Texas, I have been able to complete a second book. I know my calling with Mother Teresa will never end, since her invitation was open-ended.

Another auspicious conversation on an airplane inspired me to continue this multi-media project, despite numerous obstacles. Back in August, 1995, two months after I first met Mother Teresa in Atlanta, Georgia, while on a flight to Mumbai, an angel sat next to me and told me that I was about to embark on a project that would become my calling. He told me, "You must never give this up. Never. It is your calling."

Captured with Mother Teresa
Photograph by Sally Martin

Prophetess of Our Time

I'm not sure when these chance conversations directing my life will end. Perhaps the last one I have will be with Mother Teresa when she helps me cross over to the other side. Oh, that she would be with me at that moment of transition!

During our Rome pilgrimage in December, 2012, my son Paul Snyder and I visited the Vatican and the sanctuary of the Sistine Chapel. When we came across Michelangelo's **Birth of Creation,** we gazed in awe and wonder at the image of God reaching out to Adam and breathing life into him. Michelangelo depicts God's hand connecting to Adam's in one of the most intimate moments of all time.

This intimacy of the Holy Spirit being infused into the soul is, for me, the best way to describe my first encounter with Mother Teresa at the Atlanta Hartsfield Airport back in 1995. For me it seems as if God's loving hand reached down from heaven that day and through Mother Teresa, he touched me in a way I had never been touched before. It was the kiss of life, and as Mother Teresa looked into my eyes for our first silent conversation, I felt lifted into a place of peace and love. I was given a gift that gave me insight into the meaning of life, filling me with hope for more moments of grace. My tired body was infused with energy and I felt spiritually renewed.

She invited me to join her on that journey that began for her on the train ride to Darjeeling, India in 1947, when she received "the call within the call" to leave the Loretto Order to create her own order, the Missionaries of Charity. Mother Teresa's new apostolate would be born on the garbage piles of the poorest slums of Kolkata. The Holy Spirit invited her to participate in this life-long work to serve the destitute and impoverished, and to minister to those in the wealthiest suburbs of the world, where the well of loneliness could never be filled without the loving touch of a human hand.

The Holy Spirit breathed life into her receptive soul to give dignity and love to those who had been debased and degraded and to the millions of desperate souls littering the streets and railroad tracks of the world. When she invited me to see the work in India, I knew it was the invitation I had been waiting for all of my life. I said, "yes" and have continued this pilgrimage on a journey that has no end.

Mother Teresa and I did not have a conversation that early morning on the tarmac of the airport where we first met. When she walked up to me and enfolded my hands in her own, she peered right into my soul and simply whispered in my heart, "Come follow me." My first book takes the readers into the world of Mother Teresa at the heart of her mission in Kolkata, where she first began serving the destitute in 1950.

For six months I lived partly in her world, starting with caring for the orphans and then at Kalighat, the first home Mother Teresa established to care for the sick and dying. The home was ironically within the walls of a Hindu temple dedicated to the Goddess Kali. This blending of faiths is so iconic of Mother Teresa's mission! Although I have been deeply criticized by some readers for pointing out Mother Teresa's ecumenical mission, I would suggest that no other mission in the world draws volunteers from so many faiths to work at homes established by a Catholic order.

In all the months I spent working and socializing with other volunteers, I never once found animosity or divisiveness over faith or personal beliefs. I would speculate that the reason is quite simple. When the hands are busy caring for children, the old and dying, there is very little time or energy to spark flames of hate and animosity with each other. The feeling within the homes is quite magical; all of them share a pervasive sense of oneness. Every one of Mother's Teresa's homes is marked on the outside with a unique illus-

tration depicting the crucified Jesus and the painted words "I Thirst."

Contained in this mission of quenching the thirst of Jesus through loving hands and service, is a very simple philosophy that has continued since Mother Teresa's death. As a sister said to me in Rome over Christmas, "Mother always said, 'the work will continue without me, because it is not my work. It is God's work.'" She also told me that each of the sisters had a personal calling within the order that was completely separate from Mother Teresa's calling. "We are not trying to be Mother Teresa," she said.

When Mother Teresa finally gave me permission to document the work of the Missionaries of Charity, she again invited me to "come and see." Seated alone with her on the infamous concrete bench in the expansive hallway of the Mother House, I was shocked by the invitation to also become a nun with her order. "No Mother, I am a journalist. I don't want to be a nun." "Oh yes," she responded almost slyly, then asked "How do you spell your name?" And with that stamp of approval within a note giving me permission to photograph the work, I felt deeply rooted to her cause. However, as the Sister Marise Therese told me, "We have not been chosen to be like Mother Teresa."

Today, Mother Teresa remains quietly shrouded within the mysterious folds of her blue and white sari, as the administrators of her cause of canonization seek to establish a second miracle that will elevate her to sainthood. The two offices for her cause in Tijuana and Rome keep an ever-vigilant protective eye over the documents and letters that support the process of scrutiny and overwhelming research needed to convince the Vatican, and ultimately the Pope, that Mother Teresa is indeed deserving of canonization.

I traveled to Tijuana in the fall of 2012 to visit the shrine dedicated to Mother Teresa, as well as the homes established by her order. The photographs and video conversations of

Mother and child on the Tijuana border 2012

that visit will be shared in a third publication.

After the publication of **Mother Teresa, Come be my Light**, edited by Brian Kolodiej-chuk, M.C. -- a collection of Mother Teresa's personal letters to her confessors and superiors, in which she described feelings of the absence of God -- *Time* magazine published an article describing Mother Teresa's 'Crisis of Faith.' Suddenly devoted followers from around the world were unsettled, believing that Mother Teresa lost her faith in God. I have had many conversations in which people asked me, "Did Mother Teresa really stop believing in God?"

I was amazed by the limited research in *Time*'s article on Mother Teresa's "Dark Night of the Soul" experience. The article only quoted one priest, Fr. Van der Peet, who was one of many of Mother Teresa's priest friends, but he had limited theological experience with the dark night. I would later interview Father Van der Peet myself. He was an artistic and creative spiritual mentor for many young seminarians in Wisconsin. Fr. Van der Peet's experience with Mother Teresa was limited to letters that, while conveying some of her battle with the responsibility of heading such an enormous mission, did not reveal the inner turmoil of her human heart.

I am not a theologian, merely an avid reader of Mother Teresa materials. Long before her letters were published, I had already accessed most of them through a friend. In trying to understand that experience, I read excerpts from John of the Cross and other saints who wrote extensively about a similar journey of faith. The depths of spiritual warfare and anguish the human soul can actually tolerate without having a complete nervous breakdown continues to fascinate me.

I see that as human beings we each have a particular calling to fulfill. The Holy Spirit comes in a unique way to those souls who are willing to give up everything familiar, and to sacrifice every comfort known to man in order to serve God. Later, in the closing of this book, I will quote a sister I met in Rome on Christmas Day, who summarized the future of the church and how the working of the Holy Spirit must be free to move through our souls.

Most of us are not chosen for such an arduous journey, but we can all be called to our own special level of spirituality. I think that many people have suffered greatly through their lives and have learned profound lessons from these crises. I believe in a loving God who gives us great lessons through trials that can often lead to temporary darkness. God sometimes removes his grace, which is the light by which we see faith; we then flounder in the dark, unable to see or feel God's presence. Holding on to our faith through sheer determination, we're stripped of our pride and self-reliance, and our faith is strengthened, drawing us into a closer relationship with Christ.

Mother Teresa praying in Sacred Heart Church in downtown Atlanta, 1995

In Mother Teresa's case, her journey to Christ was often scorched by the emptiness that was once filled with light. When the attention was withdrawn, she hungered to be filled again with that heavenly awakened and tangible spirit that had become so familiar to her in the early days. While waiting hopefully, she quenched the thirst of those she had been directed to serve. I'm certain in her death, if not beforehand, she became one with her beloved Christ. That is the ultimate grace of "the Dark Night of the Soul."

As Fr. Benedict Groeschel said to me in our conversation, "Mother Teresa always had faith in God, she just didn't always have faith in herself." Msgr. John Esseff advised me that darkness is always followed by light. He told me in our conversation, "Remember Linda, that for every desolation, you will experience equal consolation. It is a spiritual law."

It was Monsignor Esseff who would help me understand that much of the suffering I had experienced was part of this process of soul cleansing. He would also enlighten me on how my gifts could serve to help others understand the way Mother Teresa viewed the world. "You have a gift of seeing the poor, Linda. Through your photographs, you are showing the world that Mother Teresa saw Christ in the poor."

I found this little girl sweeping the apartment of an abandoned building in Brooklyn, New York in 1982

Since I was a young child living in Portugal, I became familiar with those faces that lived in the nearby forest and would often come by our house begging for food, clothing and money. They were gypsies who lived in tents propped between trees off the coast of Carcavelos. Without my parents' knowledge, I would often wander into the forest to greet these roving gypsies.

Later, as a photography student at The University of Michigan, my main focus would continue to be the poor and abandoned people of the world. After graduating, I moved to New York City. I was able to explore the darkest corners of the city, meeting homeless men on the Bowery, who allowed me to photograph them. I continued this exploration in abandoned buildings in Brooklyn where I found homeless people living in the midst of unbelievable sadness.

I moved to Atlanta, Georgia in the early 1980s and was first assigned to photograph soup kitchens over Thanksgiving; I found it a privilege to be among the destitute. I never considered myself taking advantage of the poor when I took their photographs. Instead I considered it an honor that I was allowed to have a window into their world. In my experience, the Missionaries of Charity organization frowns on photographs taken within

Shazam was a homeless man living on the Bowery of New York City in 1982. He said his lifestyle was a choice.

their facilities. I understand their concern, as some charitable organizations and photographers misuse the images for personal advantage.

I truly believe Mother Teresa knew my intentions were pure, otherwise she would not have given me permission to take photographs of her work in Kolkata.

The St. Francis Prayer, which was Mother Teresa's favorite prayer for the poor, resonates profoundly in my own heart. I have never profited from the poor, otherwise I'm certain my life would have been more prosperous. There were times when Paul was young and I worried incessantly about how I was going to pay the bills each month, even though I stayed busy lecturing and selling books all over the country. The money I brought in from these engagements barely covered my bills. However, each time I saw a glowing face in the audience, I knew that Mother Teresa was coming alive at that moment in the room, and the work she had spread across the globe was not hidden in some secret convent or house for only a select few to experience. In another conversation I had with Monsignor Esseff, who was then the spiritual director for the contemplative branch of the Missionaries of Charity, he said, "Mother was like the perfect combination of the dove and the snake. You, Linda, must become more like that." Later he explained that I hadn't yet developed the practical wisdom that Mother Teresa so clearly emobodied, even though he suggested I was as compassionate as the whitest dove.

Over the years since I began my Mother Teresa journey, which has been key to my spiritual quest, I have been given new glimpses of additional facets of the "diamond" Mother Teresa reflected to the world. Each has its own persona and within that brilliance, I have found priceless sources of inspiration.

Pope Benedict named this the "Year of Faith." In the pages of this book, I will take you to Italy, first to the beatification of Mother Teresa in 2003, and then to New York, where I had a wonderful conversation with a very holy man who knew Mother Teresa for 33 years, Father Benedict Groeschel.

Father Groeschel, founder of the order of the Franciscan Friars of the Renewal, has been a counselor and teacher, and has written many books. He has been an outspoken advocate for the poor, helping found the Good Counsel Homes for homeless pregnant women, as well as the St. Francis House for young men. The mission of the Franciscan Friars of the Renewal is to preach reform and serve the poor.

Fr. Groeschel testified for the cause of Mother Teresa's beatification, and in our interview, he shared many insights into the process, including some of the conflicting testimony that wasn't favorable. The intention of the interview was to focus on Mother Teresa, yet I learned so much more – about the life of a man whose mission in life was so similar to that of Mother Teresa. He hoped to make the Catholic faith a well of nourishment for his audiences and to strictly follow the early orthodox teachings on obedience, duty and tradition as benchmarks for the future instead of as meaningless teachings of the past.

Monsignor John Esseff is a second prominent priest whom I have already mentioned. I was able to interview this Jesuit priest in Dalton, Pennsylvania, where he served at that time as the spiritual director for seminarians at the St. Pius seminary. He had once been the Pontifical appointee to Lebanon in the 1980s, and it is there where he first met Mother Teresa's sisters.

As I mentioned, all my major interviews began as a result of so called "chance" conversations. After Mother Teresa's Beatification, I traveled to Scranton, Pennsylvania with my publisher to speak at a number of venues. After one of my talks, a woman who later described herself as "the widow in the Bible," came up to me during the book-signing and in her loud and boisterous voice, insisted that I meet Msgr. Esseff, since, according to Barbara Yanchek, he knew her "better than anyone in the world." Generally I feel tired after a talk, so I didn't give much heed to this woman's suggestions.

But after I returned to Atlanta, she called me several times and insisted that I call Msgr. Esseff. Finally acquiescing, I recall the day when I called the aging priest; he answered the phone in almost a whisper. His voice was so soothing and calming to the soul that tears rolled down my cheek as we began talking about Mother Teresa. He had attended the beatification and insisted that together we should go to the canonization. He also suggested I fly to Pennsylvania and spend a few days at the seminary. I agreed instantly and booked tickets that day.

Msgr. Esseff and I would have a longer and more sustaining relationship than the one I had with Father Groeschel. On our first meeting in Pennsylvania, Monsignor agreed to be my son's godfather and my spiritual counselor. It began on a snowy morning at the seminary when I awoke from a deep sleep, dressed in blue jeans, and headed down to the cafeteria for breakfast and to await my first meeting with Msgr. Esseff. I sat down at the table with another priest, and within moments, an older gentleman in his seventies appeared near our table dressed in sweat pants. He was short with a gray beard and kindly eyes; this was Msgr. Esseff. He asked me how I had slept, and I responded "Fine. I'm very good." We both went towards the breakfast buffet and chose some healthy breakfast items and the most important part of breakfast – coffee.

After we sat down, I was planning to begin my interview by casually asking him how he met Mother Teresa. Instead, he looked steadily in my eyes and said, "So tell me about your time with Mother Teresa." I looked at him with surprise. I was not used to being asked about myself. "But I am here to ask you about her." He kindly replied, "I would like to hear your story first, Linda."

When I began to tell him my story, tears welled up in my eyes. I tried to prevent the tears, but the trickle began spontaneously and turned into a deluge. "Don't worry. He has that effect on people," advised the other priest sitting at the table. That is how my day began with Monsignor Esseff—in a seminary cafeteria in Dalton, Pennsylvania.

Two years later, Monsignor Esseff came to Atlanta, and together we addressed the entire student body of St. Pius Catholic High School. He also consecrated my house to Mother Mary during a Mass the evening before in my living room, attended by many of the people I had met during my talks in the surrounding area. Paul assisted him in the Mass, and it was clear that a sense of holiness had settled over the packed room.

The encounters I had with Mother Teresa are multi-faceted. This book is in part a collection of two conversations with two very distinct priests and the way in which at various times our lives converged as a result of our unique relationships with the great humanitarian. My conversations with these two prolific priests are wrapped around the walls of an ancient city, the center of the Catholic faith and where the cause of Mother Teresa's canonization continues in discreet whispers. This is the city where I also have a history. I now take you to Rome, Italy 2003 for the beatification of Mother Teresa.

Monsignor Esseff, Paul and I posing with a group of St. Pius students after we spoke for the entire student body in Atlanta, Ga.

St. Peter pointing the way at St. Peter's Square

Completing a book and traveling to Rome, 2003

Two thousand and three was an auspicious year for me. After many years of dedicated work as a photographer, I was now witnessing the release of my book *Come and See: A Photojournalist's Journey into the World of Mother Teresa.* It was a dream consistent with my childhood; I loved drawing pictures and captions to accompany the many books I planned to write one day. Only God could have assigned me a calling so profound and humbling -- to one day meet a living saint and be given permission by her to document the work of her order in India.

Seven months after my son Paul was born September 23, 1996, I began compiling my notes and images into a manuscript. I completed the work with steady and inspired determination in my Atlanta apartment, urged by an inner voice to move forward with the project. In 2002 I met my publisher and in less than one year two printings of the book were completed in Singapore and Thailand. The publisher, DC Press, released the coffee-table style photography book in the fall of 2003, just in time for Mother Teresa's beatification.

As soon as I heard about the beatification ceremony for Mother Teresa, which was scheduled on October 19, 2003, in Rome, I began searching for a group from the United States that might be planning a pilgrimage to the event. I discovered that a group from the Diocese of Charlotte, North Carolina was in the process of being formed, and would be headed up by retired Bishop William Curlin. I quickly made arrangements to join the pilgrimage and began to plan this new, exciting adventure.

I made childcare arrangements for Paul, while wishing he could accompany me on this journey. That would have to wait another nine years before we traveled to my beloved city together. (It will also be the final chapter of this book.)

A few days before my departure to Pennsylvania, where I would meet up with the North Carolina group, the ABC program *Good Morning America* sent a camera crew and producer to interview me for the program as part of the celebration of Mother Teresa's life. I was interviewed for over an hour, but of course only three of my quotes were used in the final program.

In the interview, I mentioned the day I had picked up a present from Mother Teresa's sisters to deliver to their leader in Kolkata. To my surprise, inside the paper bag was a box of Godiva chocolates. When I teased a sister about the chocolates she said, "Mother loves expensive chocolates." Naturally, this was one of the quotes used and viewed by millions of Americans nationwide. I was ever so slightly embarrassed to be associated with an image of Mother Teresa eating expensive chocolates in the middle of the poverty of her surroundings. Later, I would joke about the chocolate episode and tell audiences about my own associations with chocolate.

For instance, earlier I referred to an angel on my 1995 flight to Mumbai, India. The airline attendants kept bringing my flight companion expensive chocolates. He said to me, "You must always be sweet like me. See, they bring me expensive Swiss chocolates." This angel would also predict the birth of my son within a short time and as I noted earlier, he warned me that I should never give up the Mother Teresa project. He confirmed that this would be a calling filled with challenges.

Bishop Curlin leading our group in Italy for the beatification of Mother Teresa
Photograph by Joan Habib

So, when I was walking down the hallway of the Pennsylvania airport, I spotted a smiling Bishop Curlin. He laughed as he greeted me and said he had seen me on *Good Morning America* that morning. "I loved the remark about Mother eating Godiva chocolate."

I introduced myself to the many folks in the group, over 30 in total. I was the only non-Catholic, and for the first time felt slightly frightened by the prospect of joining what I thought might be a very orthodox group of Catholics, praying their rosaries on a daily basis and conducting themselves with disciplined aesthetic piety on the trip. Instead, I quickly discovered that this group had every intention of robustly enjoying everything Italy had to offer, including delicious food and wine.

Unfortunately, I was suffering from a severe bronchial infection and I coughed most of the flight to Rome. However, when we landed, I once again felt that sense of awe and delight by another glimpse of this splendid city. My fatigue was gone and I forgot about the coughing as we drove by bus through the streets of the city.

Bishop Willaim Curlin poses with our group after Mother Teresa's beatification, 2003

Excited pilgrims from all nations gathered in St. Peter's Square the morning Pope John Paul II beatified Mother Teresa on October 19, 2003

Bishop Curlin chose to bypass Rome for the two days before the beatification, in favor of beginning the pilgrimage in Assisi, home of the great saint who Curlin told us shared a charisma similar to Mother Teresa. I was glad I chose to accompany his tour, as our visits to the great basilicas and churches of Assisi further confirmed my lifelong love of St. Francis of Assisi.

Bishop Curlin gave several homilies in Assisi and shared with us numerous stories about his own personal encounters with Mother Teresa, beginning in Washington, D.C. in the 1980s where he served as a pastor in one of the less prosperous communities.

Curlin gave a colorful portrayal of his journey to Calcutta, now Kolkata and his first morning with Mother Teresa. He said that when he arrived at the Mother House, Mother Teresa looked at him with a gleam in her eye and said, "Would you like to see Jesus?" Curlin was taken aback and told our group that he had this vision of Jesus hiding in the closet of Mother Teresa's office. Instead, she invited him to "Come and see." They walked out onto the streets of Kolkata and it wasn't too far before they came upon a man dying on the sidewalk, curled up in pain. Mother Teresa knelt on the sidewalk and looking up at Curlin said, "This is Jesus."

On another occasion, Curlin said that he went to the Kalighat home for the dying, he found Mother Teresa caring for a dying patient on the men's side of the facility. "She looked embarrassed to see me," he told us in one of the Assisi homilies. Mother was bent over a bedpan cleaning the bedsores on the emaciated body of a patient. "It is as if she didn't want to see me in this situation," he said. Curlin pointed out Mother Teresa's great humility in her ability to put her words into action instead of only speaking of compassion.

Our pilgrimage group, made up of 28 parishioners, five priests, Bishop Curlin and myself, prepared ourselves for the highlight of the journey—the trip to Rome and the beatification of Mother Teresa at St. Peter's Square.

When we arrived at our destination, the Hotel Michelangelo, there was a note for me from Cable News Network requesting my presence in the skybox during the ceremonies the following day. I was surprised by this request since I hadn't been in contact with CNN regarding my whereabouts. Even though I only had one interview scheduled with NPR Radio that day, to my surprise, I was included in numerous broadcasts, including the BBC and Sky Television.

Despite the weather forecast, the next morning was crisp and beautiful, with a clear blue October sky. I jumped out from under my sky blue comforter, and opened the old-fashioned stand-alone closet door to pull out my navy blue suit. I was going to be appearing live that morning on CNN, and I already knew dark blue worked well on camera. It was also the color chosen by Mother Teresa for the identifiable blue and white striped sari uniforms, inspired by Mother Mary.

I joined my group for a hurried breakfast in the expansive dining area of the hotel. I loved the maroon velvet drapes that covered the tall windows and the gigantic chandeliers that graced the ceilings throughout the hotel. Strong coffee and croissants is the staple of the Roman breakfast diet; the buffet also offered fresh rolls with assorted cheese and salami.

That morning I was on a mission. My cheeks already were heated by my inner excitement for the coming day. I exited the hotel with a Nikon on one shoulder and a Canon video camera on the other shoulder. A heavy bag contained assorted lenses, pens and a notebook.

It was 5:30 a.m. when we arrived at the entrance to St. Peter's Square. There was a look of urgency on the immense sea of faces, filled with an intense desire to find a good vantage point inside the square. Later, Msgr. Esseff would tell me that he had been offered a VIP position close to Pope John Paul II where all the cardinals and bishops would gather.

Instead, he chose to sit with his group in crowded quarters in the middle of the square, even though the view was far less advantageous. Msgr. Esseff said he learned the lesson of humility from Mother Teresa. He told me that she had once said, "Never see yourself above or below anyone."

On the other hand, I was blessed with an entirely different vantage point that day. While my group followed our tour guide and Bishop Curlin, I met the CNN assistant producer near the magazine stand inside the square. She led me up the stairwell to the rooftop of a stately mansion. A crew of technical support team had already been working for hours making sure the live feed would proceed without interruption.

I was introduced to the smiling European correspondent and anchor and given a schedule of the morning's guests. I had about 30 minutes to relax, drink coffee and most importantly, take in the mystical celebration of this extremely holy day in the Catholic Church that would be shared with audiences worldwide.

I walked over to the edge of the rooftop with my steaming cup of coffee and could hardly believe the role I was given at that moment. In a flash, I saw a quick review of my life and how my personal calling as an artist and journalist had led me to Mother Teresa. Never would I have dreamt that evenings spent photographing homeless couples in the basements of New York City would lead to photographing Mother Teresa's lepers in a colony she founded outside Kolkata.

I had led a difficult life as an adult, compared to the standards of most of those with whom I grew up with in the wealthy suburbs of Europe and Brazil. I married a man who suffered from one of the most rare and painful cancers known to mankind. I was widowed in 1992 but was given a stunning gift to counter balance the emotional tragedies of my life – the magical encounter with Mother Teresa in 1995 in Atlanta, Georgia. She sent an arrow of love straight into my heart and it melted like the candy of heaven through my veins.

At that moment, everything made sense. The pain, the abandonment, the suffering were all part of the plan. She recognized that pain in my heart and knew this pain would help me recognize it in others and be able to convey it through my photographs and stories.

As I braced my body against the ancient stone balcony wall, tears danced on my eyelashes. I had a quick vision of my house in Atlanta where my beautiful seven year old son Paul would be sitting in the living room with our babysitter, watching a view on his television screen similar to the one I was now witnessing from my birds-eye perch overlooking the square packed in with 300,000 people. I was awed beyond belief. I couldn't have asked for a better view; it was simply breathtaking.

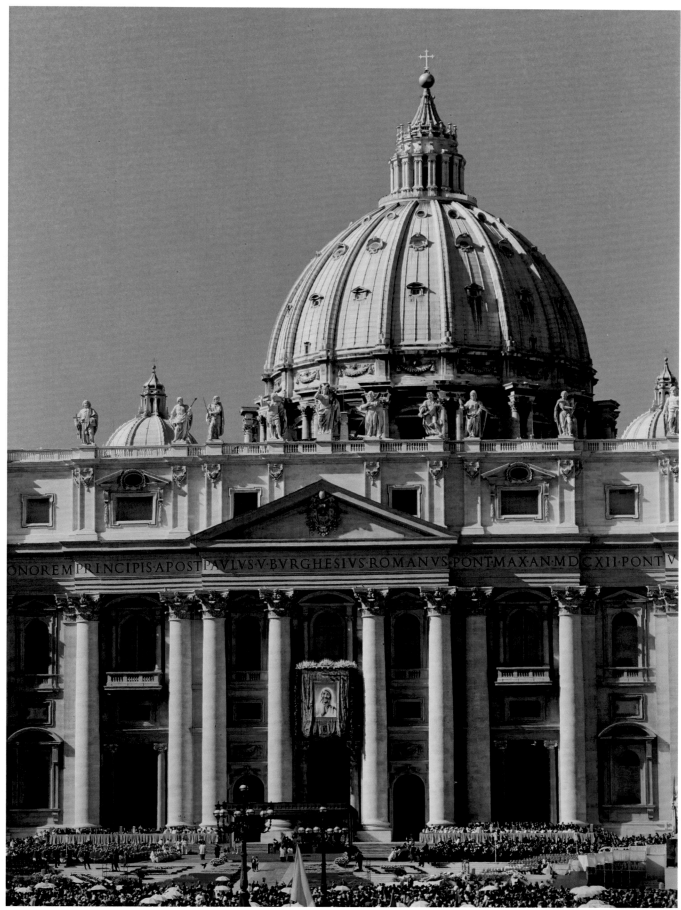

Within moments, I lifted my cameras, one at a time to record Pope John Paul being transported into the square. His golden robes fell over his very frail body, and it was clear to me at that moment that the head of the Catholic Church was taking his last breaths of life. I had named my son for the Holy Father after a magical encounter I had with him in 1981. I was living in New York City shortly before I entered graduate school at New York University. During the day I worked for commercial photographers and at night I worked as a waitress. As a struggling photographer in the city, one learns multiple survival skills just to survive.

I had rented a room in a SOHO loft on the corner of Mercer and Broad Street. Since I had worked very late the night before, I was sleeping in past 9 a.m. when I was awakened by the mixed sounds of horns blaring and voices shouting in joy. At first, I thought I was dreaming and rolled over to the other side of the bed. The voices became more urgent and the car sounds were by now, very close to my apartment. I jumped out of my Futon bed, ran to the window, peeled back the black piece of cloth covering the glass and lifted the window. To my utter shock, I saw hundreds of people crowding Mercer Street, while others were hanging off rooftops. I looked straight down to the street below and then to my amazement and incomprehension, I was looking face-to-face with Pope John Paul II. He opened his arms to me in a blessing and smiled. The twinkle in his eyes shot a dart into my soul and I felt like a drunken sailor who has been washed overboard by a giant wave.

"It's the Pope," I whispered to myself. I walked in a swoon to the middle of my apartment floor and sat cross-legged staring at the shiny wooden surface. My mind was blank. I continued to sway from side to side until the wave splashed to shore and settled into the sand. I was tingling all over from the encounter, and throughout the day I walked as if in a dream. It was very similar to the impact Mother Teresa had on me many years later on June 15, 1995.

And now here I was on a rooftop overlooking St. Peter's Square, witness to a glorious event in which Pope John Paul was lifting Mother Teresa to the altars of heaven. For the first time, I felt that I, too, was being called to the church and once again, I said, "Yes." When I returned to Atlanta, my son and I joined the Catholic Church at our local parish in Dunwoody, a suburb of Atlanta.

An assistant producer calling me to the anchor box broke my reverie. Other guest speakers were mingling around a monitor where they could view the live proceedings. I was given a seat across from the anchor as I wiped away a remaining tear. I breathed in deeply, and then moments later, I was live on CNN! For the life of me, I can barely recall that conversation, but later I heard that I did very well. My son saw me on his television set, and later when he met me at the airport, he said, "I saw you on TV Mom! I would like to join the church." And so we did.

After my "15 minutes of fame" on CNN, I returned to my position alone on the balcony and arrived in time to watch as the maroon curtain was parted, revealing an image of the now Blessed Teresa of Calcutta. It was a reverent moment. The mesmerized crowd was silent, until the smiling photograph of Teresa emerged, causing them to erupt in cheers and shouts of joy.

The BBC worldwide had asked me to appear live shortly after the ceremonies. I struggled once again, as I walked through the crowds to the European makeshift platform built days before in the back of the square. For the remainder of the day I appeared on various newscasts in a dreamlike state. That night, as we prepared to travel back to the United States, I thought my journey with Mother Teresa was over, until I encountered "Mr. Hugo" on the Alitalia return flight to the United States.

On the road as a speaker and author

And then came my encounter with the pushy, loud friend of Msgr. Esseff at a book signing in the Scranton, Pennsylvania area. It was at one of the parishes that I met Barbara Yanchek, who had a tremendous devotion to Mother Teresa. Barbara marked a spot for herself next to the table where I had been set up to sign books. She had accompanied Monsignor John Esseff to Rome for the beatification, and as I've said she insisted that I absolutely had to meet him. "He knew Mother Teresa better than anyone," she told me in her strong and loud Pennsylvania accent.

I was still suffering from bronchitis, and I desperately tried to hide behind my books, wanting to be left alone. I was feeling considerably weaker by this time, and the constant travel and speaking had left me quite fragile. The bronchitis hung onto me like a ruthless demon; my lungs were filled with fluid and the coughing had been keeping me awake most nights. In fact, by this time I was so tired and sick, I was unable to distinguish between a physical fever and the spiritual fever of my mission; everything simply blurred together.

Speaking for a Catholic women's group in Hilton Head, South Carolina.

Sharing Mother Teresa's life with students at St. Neumann Catholic School in Florida

The day after this engagement, my publisher drove me in his rental car through the snowy landscape of rural Pennsylvania to meet his investors. We gathered at a middle-class diner near Allen, Pennsylvania and I faced a group of extremely wealthy and very friendly Catholics. I was once again asked to give a personal account of my time with Mother Teresa. Afterwards, as the listeners came to greet me, they spontaneously would reach out and hug me; by this time, I was becoming used to being touched. It was as if somehow they felt I was connected to Mother Teresa through my flesh. Later an orthodox Catholic told me I was a fourth-class relic since I had been touched by Mother Teresa!

I finally had a respite from my travels, although I still hadn't seen a doctor. Somehow I bypassed this bout of illness without antibiotics, and slowly the coughing ceased and I began to feel stronger. Thankfully, as a string of speaking engagements kept me quite busy for the next four years.

In the meantime, another book was hatching, and Barbara was surely an instrument. She called me at least three more times from Pennsylvania. As a result of her persistence, I finally called Monsignor Esseff. As I mentioned earlier, our encounter at the seminary in Pennsylvania was absolutely riveting.

Conversation with Monsignor John Esseff
Dalton, Pa. ~ St. Pius X Seminary

Monsignor Esseff stationed in Beirut, Lebanon

After our breakfast in the seminary cafeteria, we walked to Msgr. Esseff's office, where a sense of deep tranquility prevailed. One wall was lined with 8x10 frames that were inexpensive, but filled with mesmerizing and priceless images. I beheld Monsignor photographed with Pope John Paul II, Monsignor with Mother Teresa in Kolkata; and photographs from parishes within a war-torn Lebanon in the 1980s.

As I took time to scan the images, Monsignor quietly gazed at me. Before we began our four hour videotaped interview, Monsignor knew more about me in a few minutes than I would ever know about him. He shared so much of Mother Teresa's sensibilities and innate intuitiveness.

He sensed a nervous mannerism that normally I am able to hide from less keen eyes.

"Why are you worried Linda?" he asked me as I was setting up the camera.
"Well, I don't normally leave my son for this long a period of time," I responded.
"Do you think that God wants you to be here Linda?" Taken aback by this line of questioning, I thought about it for a moment and nodded my head. "So, if God wants you to be here, do you not think that he is taking care of Paul?" he asked me.

Again, not even an hour since breakfast, I felt hot tears filling my eyes.
"Linda, God is in control. Why don't you surrender to this moment, and let God take care of Paul?" No one had ever spoken to me like this before. I had grown up in such a con-

trolling environment, but in reality there was no control or faith within those vulnerable walls, only insecurity and uncertainty.

His words lifted the heaviness that was weighing me down, and I sighed with relief letting my guard down and allowing myself to fully participate in the conversation with Msgr. Esseff. We spent the entire day together and decided to spend the following morning visiting some of the venues where he ministered, including the prison.

That night, the snow blew against my bedroom window as if to make entry into the tiny seminarian room. I enjoyed the sounds of swirling snow and wind, as I lay snuggled into the folds of my warm blankets. I fell into a deep and rare, worry-free sleep.

The next morning Msgr. Esseff met me again in the cafeteria, dressed in gray sweat pants. I was dressed in the usual blue jeans and a white wool sweater. He walked up to my table and smiled. "You look like Mary right now Linda." I was growing accustomed to his kind remarks.

I had come prepared to drive through the snowy, ice-encrusted streets of Scranton but Monsignor had other plans. "I was talking to Mother this morning, Linda," he began. "I think we are going to do something else. Mother told me that you need to spend some time with Jesus." (Monsignor often talked to Mother Teresa and simply called her "Mother"). I looked at Monsignor with alarm; "What the heck does he mean by that?" I wondered. "Come," he said.

Mother Teresa and Monsignor Esseff

We walked to a tiny chapel across from his office and he guided me to the first pew. "I think you need to develop a relationship with Jesus," he advised. For the next hour we spoke about my childhood and my relationship to the church and God. "You have tried every bottle on the shelf Linda." referring to my journeys to ashrams in India and efforts to be affiliated with various churches. "Now it is time to know Jesus. I am going to leave you in this room for a couple hours. Stay here until I come back."

That is where I spent the second morning in St. Pius Seminary—in a tiny chapel facing the figure of Christ dying on the cross. I did not hear Jesus speaking to me, but I did feel an ethereal sense of wonder and peace the remainder of the weekend. As I mentioned earlier, my relationship with Monsignor would become tightly bound through our faith, through our similar devotion to Mother Teresa and through my son.

Our taped interview began first with a prayer and a Hail Mary. Together we said, "Hail Mary, full of grace. The Lord is with thee. Blessed art thou among women, and blessed is the fruit of thy womb, Jesus."

Esseff: Between heaven and earth, that is my role as a priest. I see so many poor, needy and suffering people; I take them to God. I see that as my role as a priest. Much of the priest's life is with God. He goes to God on behalf of the people. But it is also to know God and to praise Him as well as to intercede on behalf of people. When he comes from God he goes to the people. I really do believe that I am called to be Christ to people; I am called to be Jesus. Mother used to have that feeling, but for everyone. You are called to be Christ. So everyone I meet is Christ.

Schaefer: Monsignor, can you tell when you first met Mother Teresa?

Esseff: Yes. I was stationed in Beirut, Lebanon and Mother had established a center for the Missionary of Charity sisters in Sid el Bausheria. Lebanon in those days was a hell-hole. There was constant bombardment, constant suffering and shelling. It is the first time I had been in a war. I had seen a lot of poverty when I had my five years in South America in Peru. But that was one of my first experiences of war. Everyday was shelling and car bomb blasts and you didn't know when it was going to happen.

In the center of Beirut is a section known as Sid el Bausheria. A group of seven sisters were established there. At this time, most English-speaking sisters had left the area and there were only a few of us Jesuits who offered Mass for the sisters. I was stationed as the director of the Pontifical Mission for Palestine in a section of Beirut. It was not much of a drive for my driver to take me to the Missionary of Charity sisters so I could give Mass.

From my seat, huddled over my camera, I gazed at the wall that depicted some photographs of Msgr. Esseff with Mother Teresa's sisters, who would one day become her legacy. As Monsignor described these early encounters in Beirut, it was as though I was traveling there with him and participating in these special Masses amidst the turbulence and violence of Beirut.

Esseff: It was not very long before I met the most amazing and extraordinary group of women I had ever met in my life. I was sent to Lebanon in 1984. I was ordained in 1953, so I was a priest for over 30 years at this time. But I had never met a group of women so

Mother Teresa 1975 in Rome; photograph by Father Van der Peet

in love with our Lord. That little convent of theirs was so filled with peace and love; it just radiated with joy. They were really in touch with the poorest of the poor.

I've been inside a lot of convents where there were conflicts at times, but these sisters were so hungry for Jesus and they were so filled with joy. I had never met a group like this. They were from India, the Philippines and from Yugoslavia at that time. I always remember them as loving and radiating Christ. So when I talked to them it was like we just "hit it off," as they say. I was looking for this kind of person and somehow they were looking for me. We fit together.

Monsignor began giving the sisters day retreats and days of recollection. His role as the Director of the Pontifical Mission required that he travel back and forth to Rome. By this time, the sisters had told Mother Teresa about Monsignor Esseff. She enquired through the sisters, whether he could lead a retreat in Rome for the junior sisters who were about to make their profession.

Esseff: *When I got to Rome, she said, "No, I want you to talk to my superiors." The superiors were having a retreat in Rome. That was my first meeting with Mother.*

I was enjoying this open conversation and impressed by Monsignor's frankness. I was so accustomed to religious discussions being tempered by tactfulness and political correctness. From what I heard in the community, Monsignor had a reputation for being very direct, and speaking his mind, even if it meant ruffling a few feathers. Later, I would learn Father Groeschel shared that quality of straightforwardness. However, Monsignor's first conversation with Mother Teresa did surprise me.

Esseff: *I said, "You know Mother, I'm not impressed by people I read about. So often they are so disappointing. When I meet them I am usually disappointed. It wasn't you I was looking forward to meeting. When I met your sisters, your daughters, I was bowled over because they truly were Christ living in the world. They radiated this love and this joy."*

I often tell the sisters that the greatest gift Mother Teresa has given to the world are the sisters. It was a community who were in love with our Lord and a community in love with the poorest of the poor. It was under the direction and guidance and inspiration of our Lord. When they gave me their rule of life, I was so amazed. These sisters would leave home for ten years and not go back. I never met a group like that. If your father died while you are on mission, well, you pray for him and you would grieve. And that would happen to some of them. A parent would die. But they're commitment and their dedication; their holiness; their aestheticism...This was a new wave of love. This was a beach-

Volunteer with children from Shishu Bhavan in Kolkata, India 1995

38

head for God. The war was all around them, but when I went into their convent (The House of Peace) I'd come in from the war from seeing the suffering and pain and enter their home and it was a haven of peace and joy.

Schaefer: What was in there?

Esseff: Children, retarded, and cast-offs—only the people who didn't want their babies, sent them there. They were malformed, ill-formed, all kinds of deformities. When you saw the sisters in the nursery, caring for them, I knew that was Jesus in that baby. They would hold them, love them and sing to them. Monsignor's visits to the home to offer Mass also became an opportunity for members of the community to find a sanctuary within the peaceful walls.

That initial meeting with Mother Teresa in Rome became the beginning of a long relationship between Monsignor Esseff and the Missionaries of Charity. Monsignor explained to me that the sisters became known as a conservative order. However, he also said they were unique and hard to categorize. He quickly developed a reverence and sense of awe for Mother Teresa and her sisters.

Esseff: I see them as the most authentic group of sisters; they are so powerful. They don't fit some of those categories at all. Remember I was telling you that to be a disciple of Christ you must be as gentle as a dove and as cunning as a snake. Mother had both those qualities. She was such a combination. The Holy Father called her the greatest missionary of the 20th century. She was so powerful in her generosity but also in her wisdom.

Monsignor steered the conversation towards Albania, the country Mother Teresa left when she was 18 years old to join the Loretto Order in Ireland, where she would remain until the fall of communism. He described Mother Teresa's intense efforts to open a home in a country that had been under The People's Socialist Republic of Albania from 1976 until 1991. She almost failed in this attempt but through her perseverance, I came to understand Mother Teresa's central mission. It was defined by the order's total dependence and surrender to God on a daily basis. This would require an all-pervasive faith in God and in His Divine Providence. According to Monsignor, Catholics had not been to Mass in 40 years. The country was also populated by Eastern Orthodox and Muslims.

Esseff: We were in Albania and we went to seven different mission sites. Albania had been the most communist country in the world and nothing was allowed in there. Suddenly Albania has opened up and Mother is bringing her sisters into the country. I was in one of Mother Teresa's Mission Centers...Donations had been given to the home where I was giving a retreat to the sisters. Mother rarely left the Chapel, but after one of the talks, she discovered that the Superior had hoarded boxes of food and canned goods that she hadn't distributed to the poor. Mother was really fussing with the Superior, "What's going on in here?" These belong to the poor."

Mother Teresa herself began distributing the food to the long lines of poor waiting in line outside the home. She didn't stop until the pantry was empty. Msgr. Esseff told me Mother Teresa did not want to embarrass the Superior by exposing her actions. Instead, she gave the sister spiritual advice, "It's here, give it to them now, God will take care of tomorrow."

Esseff: Unbelievably, one of those U.N. trucks pulled up the next day and there were all these deliveries. They received such a huge amount of food that they wouldn't have had had a place to store the goods if they hadn't given the other food away. So that idea of "Give us this day our daily bread, just for today"... when the Hebrews were in the desert, would get just enough manna for the day. That was the spirit of poverty that she lived. Her sisters are very deeply grounded in that training. When they receive, their training is to give it away to the poor.

Monsignor's witness of this validation of Mother Teresa's faith in action in Albania, was quickly followed by another story. She had a desire to open a home in the Vatican. (Over Christmas of 2012, Paul and I would have the opportunity to visit the soup kitchen founded on Vatican grounds.)

Esseff: Mother was pretty aware, as well as anybody, of the Vatican riches but she wanted to have a home for the poor on the Vatican Grounds. She said, "Guess what Father? We're going to get a place in the Vatican! Jesus is going to come to the Vatican in the poorest of the poor." She had gone to Rome in order to do that herself, and I happened to be there at that time.

Mother Teresa had sent several sisters to meet with an Archbishop who was in charge of the Vatican properties and programs. Mother Teresa had reviewed the Vatican blueprints and had already chosen a site for her future home. Naturally, there was no easy way to get through the intricate maze of Vatican bureaucracy and her efforts were fruitless.

Esseff: She had done her homework, had scouted out the place. When she came back the sisters asked her, "Did you get it, did you get it?" Mother said, "No, we're going to pray some more." The next day she had a meeting with the Holy Father, and while they were meeting—It probably wasn't on the agenda to talk to the Holy Father about it [the home] but she asked his permission to open a home.

Mother Teresa received the Pope's blessing and signature for a home in the Vatican. When she visited the Archbishop the following day, he again said, "No." But when he saw Mother Teresa's signed paper from Pope John Paul II he said, "Well that's enough for me. You can have it."

Esseff: She believed that Jesus was in the Vatican, but He must come there every day as the poorest of the poor to be fed and clothed and cared for.

Monsignor described another powerful encounter with the Holy Father. One morning Mother Teresa was on her way to the Vatican with a group of sisters for an appointment with Pope John Paul II, when a chance encounter with a dying man on the street delayed that meeting.

Esseff: As they drove toward the Vatican, there, on the streets of Rome, they saw a poor man dying on the street.

Mother Teresa made the driver stop the car and immediately stepped out of the vehicle to attend to the man's needs. She began praying for the man and blessing him. A horrified sister said, "Mother, you are going to be late for the Pope." She said, "Tell Our Holy Father I am with Jesus."

Mother Teresa had an audience with the Holy Father only months before she died. The doctor never gave her permission to make that journey to Rome from India, but she had an inner mission that May in 1997. When she met with the Holy Father, he kissed her on the forehead and she described the moment. "He kissed me right here." He bent down and kissed her, not once but twice.

Esseff: I said, "Oh, Mother, our Holy Father loves you so much." He really loved Mother Teresa; those two were really such a pair. In ages past, you heard of different saints that clicked together, like St. Francis and St. Clare; men and women who just loved and admired each other's ministry.

I think this age will be dominated by the legacy of John Paul II and Mother Teresa. Their friendship and their love, their commitment to the Blessed Mother, to the Church and to our time, and to peace and to missions – that was a great combination for the Catholic Church in our time. There were the sexual scandals and all the things that plagued the church during this century, but then there were these two powerful figures—outstanding signs of the times. The Church had an awful lot of darkness around it but it had these two radiating figures of light.

That last encounter between Mother Teresa and Pope John Paul in Rome was six years before the Holy Father celebrated his Silver Jubilee, and shortly thereafter celebrated the beatification of Mother Teresa in St. Peter's Square. Monsignor Esseff was present on that auspicious day, seated in the middle of the square while I was perched on a rooftop viewing the spectacular scene through my Nikon lens. I captured and personally experienced an unimagineable mythic scene that truly encapsulated and defined the concept that

Madre Teresa riceve le chiavi di "Casa Allegria" - Roma, Primavalle, dal Santo Padre, Papa Giovanni Paolo II. il 23. Ottobre, 1980.

MOTHER IS RECEIVING THE KEY FROM THE HOLY FATHER POPE
JOHN PAUL II°ON THE 23/10/1980 FOR THE HOUS OF PRIMAVALLE
"CASA ALLEGRIA"ROME.

Foundation.

God uses the least among us to do His work. On that day a tiny humble nun who once washed the leper's sores was now revealed as the Blessed Teresa of Calcutta.

Esseff: When I was at her beatification and I saw the 300,000 people from all over the world and millions of people watching—here's this old man drooling, and here's this little lady less than 5 foot tall commanding the attention of the world. I thought how God uses the weak of the world and the small to confound the rest; the power that came right through, you surely couldn't say that it was them. This power of God radiates I think, through the little ones. He does choose the weak to confound the strong.

Our conversation went on a journey from Rome back to Beirut and then to Ethiopia and Eritrea. Monsignor wanted to convey to me in as short a time as possible the amazing influence Mother Teresa had on political and religious leaders of her day. During his tenure in Beirut, he described a dramatic set of events that led up to a simple solution, as a result of Mother Teresa's ability to soothe even the most powerful egos.

Esseff: This is another example of Mother's influence and directness with the powerful and mighty. When I was in Beirut, they were kidnapping Americans and had blown up the Marine barracks; there was an anti-western targeting. My superiors were very concerned and wanted to move me out of there. Archbishop O'Connor, who was Cardinal Archbishop of New York, was coming over to do a junket to focus attention on the famine victims of Ethiopia. It was in the middle 80s...He came over with a group from New York; there were photographers and people from the secular media accompanying him. When he came to Ethiopia, there were several Russian pilots who were supposed to fly us up to Eritrea.

Eritrea was at that time devastated by famine, and Cardinal O'Connor wanted to document the atrocities through the assistance of the press. However, the Russian pilots refused to fly the group of Americans. Msgr. Esseff described what happened next.

Esseff: Way off in the corner of the airport is this little lady, Mother Teresa, with about two or three of her sisters. The Cardinal Archbishop was really upset, "Who made these plans... I brought all these people, and we're not going to see anything." Mother sees what's going on and she goes right over to the pilots and there she is blessing them with God, laying her hands on their heads and giving them Miraculous Medals, and acting like a mother to these big Russian pilots. Because she spoke Slavonic she was able to talk to them in their native language. They were so thrilled to meet Mother Teresa and in ten minutes we were up in the air.

Monsignor's knowledge of international turmoil and the Church's participation in that arena was absolutely astounding. In the midst of this amphitheater of communism, war and poverty, there was Mother Teresa, soothing out tensions like a mother placating her children.

Esseff: We're all God's children...She was so simple and she went directly to the person. She saw the person; whether it was the poor in the streets or a soldier or a psychiatrist. Whoever that person was, she went right to the person.

Monsignor continued to describe Mother Teresa's relationship with communist leaders.

Esseff: There are communists in the world who so admire Mother because of her love for the poor. I have met those people; they are so dedicated to caring for the underdog, for the suffering and for the poor. They feel they can hate the rich and even go to war for the poor. But you see Mother cared for both the rich and the poor. In our world today, that combination was like an explosion.

Schaefer: This is playing the devil's advocate. Some people would say, "This is about charity. She was about helping the poor and not about changing the lives of the poor. Besides, why can't these people go out and work? Why do we have to give them food and welfare and money. Why can't they get a job?"

Addicted to heroin in Mexico, this man is fed by the Missionaries of Charity on the streets where he cleans cars to support his addiction.

Esseff: I think there are those who are going to help our society by that grace. There are those who want to change the social structures. That is an authentic view; I don't think Mother would argue with that. But she also said there was a necessity for doing a very gospel-based calling. When the Lord called her to do this work, there was someone who was needed in the world at that time to do it. There aren't that many around who are ready and willing to do it.

She became that attraction for those of us who felt called and wanted to do this work. I think there has to be that kind of community that serves the poor. There are many who are united in changing social structures so they can change societies to the extent that we don't have this great huge gap—because when the rich get richer, the poor get poorer. That's true, especially in a capitalist world.

Monsignor basically defined two groups of active supporters of the poor—those who want to change social structures through social change and government modalities, while groups such as the Missionaries of Charity are more concerned about helping those who can't help themselves through immediate assistance.

During those four hours in Msgr.'s Esseff's office, I was so focused on his gift for storytelling, that I completely lost sense of time. I glanced out the window at the expansive white snowy landscape, and then continued to tape more engaging stories about Mother Teresa, including her mission with Daniel Ortega in Nicaragua and then later a profound ending to the infamous prayer breakfast with the Clintons at the White House.

Mother Teresa was always prepared to fly into a country that needed immediate assistance. During an earthquake in the early 1980s in Nicaragua, she brought a group of sisters to assist humanitarian efforts to help those affected by the disaster. She also assisted on another project—the baptism of Daniel Ortega's children.

Esseff: Nicaragua is a very poor Central American country. When the earthquake occurred, Mother arrived with some of her sisters. Daniel Ortega, who is a communist, appeared and he was going to introduce Mother. They were (supposed to be) getting a place ready for her sisters who were helping the earthquake victims. Instead, he used the occasion to rant and rail against Ronald Reagan. "President Reagan is a Neo-Colonialist; President Reagan is a terrible person. He's here and he is taking advantage of little countries. All this economic power of America is being used to subjugate and colonize the people of Nicaragua. We are really not free...We are under the power of this system."

Mother Teresa waited patiently for her turn to address the gathering crowds. Then came the moment that can only be described as the "ingenious Mother Teresa moment." She turned and faced the president of Nicaragua and completely ignored his anti-American speech. Instead, she chose her words wisely, a manner that would become legendary.

Esseff: She said, "President Reagan really needs prayers, doesn't he?" He says, "Yes Mother, he really needs prayers." And she says, "And so do you." She said, "I understand you are a Catholic." He wasn't about to deny it. Ninety percent of this country is Catholic, or even more. He says, "Yes I am Mother." She said, "I was talking to your wife, and your seven children have not been baptized. They need that to be saved..You know that as a Catholic. I'll be their Godmother and you and I now can go down to arrange with the priest. We can have them all baptized." She said, "You know, if you can't run your family right, you can't run the country."

So, Mother Teresa became the Godmother to Daniel Ortega's seven children that day. Instead of arguing with him, she went straight to his heart as a father and as a Catholic. Next, Monsignor and I traveled to Washington, D.C. for the National Prayer Breakfast during the Clinton era. Mother Teresa was the keynote speaker. According to Msgr. Esseff, she had a great fondness for the American president…however….

Esseff: She said about our former president, "You know, his mother just didn't raise him right." She (Mother Teresa) really loved him I think; she loved Bill Clinton.

Esseff: She was invited to be the speaker at the breakfast. The courage of that woman. The president and his wife, and the vice president and his wife were present at the breakfast. They were very strongly pro-abortion and pro-choice. Mother Teresa spoke about the horrors of abortion, about the unborn and what a terrible assault and what a terrible crime it was. I still have her speech from that time. When she was finished, everyone gave her a standing ovation except the Clintons and the Gores. They just sat there.

Mother went right over to Hillary Clinton and said, "You know Mrs. Clinton, I can use your help. I want to fight abortion through adoption and I would like you to help me get a house in Washington where women who are pregnant can go and have a choice to keep their babies. I know you have the power and the influence to get such a house. If you get it, I will see to it that my sisters staff it and that they will take care of these unwed mothers."

Mrs. Clinton committed to helping Mother Teresa in that short meeting. The very next day, according to Msgr. Esseff, Mother Teresa began regularly calling Clinton, until finally her persistence paid off and a home was founded.

Esseff: Hillary Clinton was instrumental in opening a home in Washington for unwed mothers, that are now being cared for by the sisters of the Missionaries of Charity.

People would put down Hillary Clinton. Mother didn't. Mother went after the goodness

Homeless American woman living in Tijuana.

that was in everybody. She had the power to see the goodness and their capacity to help others.

Before the Clintons moved into the White House, Mother Teresa often spoke to President Ronald Reagan and never hesitated to ask for his assistance in helping the poor around the world.

Esseff: She told me this story about when Belize was in famine and the country was suffering terribly. She had this inspiration when she woke up one day to call Ronald Reagan. Something told her Reagan would help. It was very soon after, maybe within a day or two there were planeloads of food and medication going to this famished center in the world.

Monsignor relayed another story about Mother Teresa's dealing with the leaders of Albania. When she was preparing to find a home in that country shortly after the end of communism, she had a meeting with the President who promised her two homes. That promise appeared to have been placed on a back burner until Mother Teresa reminded the President of his promise. Mother Teresa knew how to overcome almost any obstacle in her path if it was central to her mission.

Esseff: She went right to the President and said, "I would like you to give me two houses." She said, " I would like two houses because the people are suffering there." He said, "This is a place Mother, where there is great poverty." Albania was terribly deprived during those years under communism. The counsel that had previously met with her had offered a huge building that was a former army barracks to take care of the poor. They had asked, "Is that what you need?" "No, I need two," she said. "One is to take care of the poor, but my sisters need a place to pray. I need a convent." She pointed out another building and said, "I want that one."

They ran into a stalemate. They were only going to give her one. She said, "The President said he would give me two. Let's stop the meeting right now." It was a big meeting...All kinds of political figures from that area. She said, "No, call the President on the phone." The president gets on the phone and he said, "Yes, she can have that building." So the new President gives Mother the place she wants.

At the end of Apartheid in South Africa, Mother Teresa immediately wanted to form a home and began asking for volunteers from among her sisters. However, she wanted to send a strong message and that would impact her final choice of who would go to South Africa after the abolishment of racial segregation.

Esseff: Mother wanted to give a sign for Apartheid. She had received permission to open a convent in South Africa; they had been waiting and praying for this. She wanted to have an integrated convent. Her sisters were thrilled when she finally got permission to do this.

51

Their hands went up to volunteer for the home, but one sister was told by Mother, "You are not black enough." She wanted the white, white and the black, black sisters...She really wanted to give them a sign.

From South Africa to Cuba, Mother Teresa knew no boundaries. She met with Fidel Castro, and her order was the first religious group allowed into the Communist dominated island.

Esseff: *She had made a reputation with the communists all around the world. I don't know if you remember the Mother House in Calcutta. Right behind the Mother House is the Communist Center. The Communists are pretty strong in India.*

Castro simply asked her, "Why do you want to come to Cuba?" She said, "I want to take care of the poor." "Mother," he said. "Welcome." See, Castro's problem was with the wealthy. He was a revolutionary and a communist who turned atheistic. Big error there. Godless. But he had a fascination and a love for the poor; he separated the love for the poor from the love for God. That, of course, is the error of communism.

He saw in Mother that authentic love for the poor; so when he was inviting her in, he wasn't bringing in an organization that was going to suck off the poor. That is what we are sometimes accused of doing...Sometimes we haven't been that authentic witness.

Monsignor himself has a great love for the poor and spoke with great passion about the manipulation of the poor by the wealthy.

Esseff: *Think of some of these places that have huge buildings laid over with gold and all kinds of donations that poor people give. There is a whole level of clergy and religion that seems to take, not really caring for the poor in their area. The Church must be concerned with the poor. It's a sign of the presence of Jesus; His love for the poor. If the Church is going to be the elongation of Christ in the world, then it must give that witness. It's people like Mother Teresa that authenticate. She had such a devotion to the Church; she loved the Church. She saw the Church as the source from which she drew her strength to serve the poor, especially in the area of salvation and evangelization. Her sisters are marvelous evangelists and teachers of the Gospels.*

Based on my experience, I suggested to Monsignor that neither Mother Teresa nor her sisters were known for actively converting non-believers to the Catholic faith.

Esseff: *Their power of conversion is that they do it by attraction rather than arguing. She lives it. That authentic living is the most powerful preaching.*

Monsignor and I had lunch in the seminary cafeteria and then had time to unwind after the long, taped conversation. I was fairly exhausted by this time, but fascinated by the journey of a faithful Catholic priest and how it coincided with the mission of a very willful nun.

After our meal, we resumed the interview. It began with the topic of the "American way," which I had determined was based on a quick-fix society. Monsignor began by sharing his thoughts on the Christian Gospel, and pointed out Mother Teresa's faithful adherence to the teachings. He gave me an abbreviated version, which I thought was important to include in this book.

Esseff: I really don't think we know what the Gospel is. Mother Teresa was a person who believed in the Gospel...and for whom the Gospel is the evangelization; she's a missionary, and she's going out to evangelize.

What is the Gospel? In the history of the world, there are two people who began it all, we believe in the one human family that came from Adam and Eve. These two people were with God and had fellowship with God. God created them as good, but through their sin and through the inspiration of the devil, they fell. That's kind of simple, but that's enough

Contemplative sisters in prayer, San Diego 2012

for now. Because of their brokenness from God, He promised that He would send a Savior and a Redeemer.

In his explanation, Msgr. Esseff said that after the fall every human being became infected with sin and it has existed as an age-old disorder in the universe for two millennium. The fall caused a disruption in God's original plan of peace and harmony for His chosen people.

Esseff: *After speaking to Adam and Eve, God did not speak again until He spoke to a wandering Armenian, Abraham, who lived somewhere in Iraq. When God spoke to this man, He said, "I am going to choose you, and from you the Redeemer will come into the world." The history of his children continued with the Hebrews and the twelve sons of Jacob, but unfortunately so did the failure of his people to adhere to his covenant.*

As a result of their disobedience, God allowed them to suffer slavery in Egypt, before freeing them. But of course the Hebrews turned their backs on God because of their refusal to believe in His omnipotence. As a result of their sin, instead of being able to enter the "Promised Land," they were forced to wander in the desert for 40 years.

Finally, God fulfilled his promise and sent His own son to be the Redeemer, born of a woman, Mary, who was full of grace. She conceived of the Holy Spirit and in Msgr. Esseff's own words "My goodness! Gracious sakes alive! God is going to fulfill this promise. God the second person became a human being, this half-crawly bug that was so diseased for all these centuries in this little planet, that's just a little piece of dust that goes around the sun."

Esseff: *So this little boy Jesus grows up, He's the Savior and we weren't nice to Him, we killed Him. We put Him on a cross and He rose from the dead. Well, He was the Savior and He was the Redeemer, He overcame death, He overcame Satan, and He broke our chain to sin and death... He came back from the dead. He's still going around with these screwballs that He had picked, Plan A, His apostles who don't know a blessed thing, they're frightened out of their wits.*

Finally He goes back to Heaven and He sends the Holy Spirit. The Holy Spirit comes on these twelve men and they are baptized. Now that's the kicker, that's what I'm really talking about. The Divine Life that was in Him comes into each one of us; each one of us that is baptized then becomes Jesus. We become Christ in the world, and we're attached and united to Him.

As Msgr. Esseff explained "that's good news"! The problem is that even though so many are baptized and united with Jesus through grace, in every heart lurks darkness and sin. Those who work hard to walk in the light are given clarity to see their faults. Those who

drift from the light are blinded and they don't see "how messed up they are, they don't see the disease and the mess and the sinfulness that's theirs, the pride, the jealousy, the egoism, the lust, and the sinfulness, they don't even see that: they're blind, but they're afraid to come into the light. Those who say, " I'm really a Christian and I'm in this Light," called to live His life." What is this life? It's to suffer and die like He did and to rise as he did." At this point I saw Msgr. Esseff's eyes fill with light.

Continuing the interview, Msgr. Esseff discussed consolation and desolation in the Rules of St. Ignatius, and described Mother Teresa as a sterling example of living in and through Jesus. (St. Ignatius describes consolation as "something happy, uplifting, which instills joy and gives peace.")

Esseff: In consolation everything is going well with the children, your job is fine, you feel great and you feel like you're just fine. Those who have extreme joy have never been happier. But after the height of your consolation will be the depths of your desolation.

Guaranteed, something terrible will happen and you're going to be so desolate, so down, so broken, when you feel lost, abandoned, confused and in turmoil. It's not bad luck, it's a (spiritual) law: to the depths of your desolation, so too will be the heights of your consolation. You know when I meet people who are in this darkness, suicidal, what a great message this is to them – you will be consoled. You will find light more brilliant than you've ever found before, just really hang in and trust that this will work out. When you are in consolation, know there's going to be desolation. Bad things happen -- your mother is going to die, you're going to get sick. After desolation comes consolation; it's a law...There will be desolation, then consolation, that's the road we all follow.

(I allowed my camera to roll and recorded Monsignor as he continued his lesson on the Rules of Ignatius' spiritual principles. I was fascinated by this elderly priest's knowledge and widespread influence in his community and around the world.)

Monsignor's insights into the nature of this saint were inspiring. Many parishioners in the Scranton community would later tell me they regarded him as a saint and cited a number of miracles in the community.

Esseff: There are the signs of the saints, like Mother, and that's what I would see with her. Every day there would be this not too high, not too low rhythm in her life. I could see her and her eyes would be sunk in. She would be so worn and so exhausted and then within hours, so filled with joy, and radiant, I would see this in her over and over again within a day. So she was coming to the end of her time, burning out with the life of Christ... her suffering and her dying and her rising until that day when she finally closes her eyes in death and she opens them up and that's the resurrection, that's exactly what Jesus did.

When I was in Rome on our last retreat I asked Mother 'So when they take and bury this body of yours, Mother what do you want me to pray for?' I came up to her; she had a paper-thin heart but her eyes were full of light. Mother said, "I want to go to China, pray I go to China before I die, I want to go to China". She had such a love and wanted (her sisters) to go to China.

Esseff: *One-fifth of the world's people are there. They haven't heard the Gospel, and she wanted to bring Jesus to the Chinese. She had so many sisters ready for China, who spoke Chinese and they were ready to go, and they still are. She didn't go because our Holy Father is holding off; I think because of the conflict between the National Church and the Patriarch Church, where they don't let the Holy Father's name in the Mass, because they don't recognize him, it's a communist regime. Jesus came for the whole world. Look where she came from, India. When I went there, I used to see them adoring a cow and all their gods, and the way they divided up the castes. But going back to the Gospel, the Gospel is our union with Christ and Christ from the beginning said, "What they've done to me, they're going to do to you." What I have gone through, you will go through, follow me."*

I asked Monsignor if the saints are expected to endure so much suffering in their spiritual and physical lives.

Esseff: *I would say we are all called to do it. The saints are such a variety of people. It is an indication that all people can do it, but it is for the hearty and it means total surrender. When Mother would see the poorest of the poor, there she would see Jesus. Did you*

The Last Supper illustrated at the Shrine of Mother Teresa in Tijuana

notice when you went to the House for the Dying, how little screaming there was or crying? That quiet way in which they would bear their sufferings, the wounds and the pus, the sufferings of their body—they weren't into a lot of self-pity or demanding attention. They reverently approached their deaths.

Since Mother Teresa founded the Missionaries of Charity in 1950, the sisters first worked out of a flat donated by a family member. Very quickly, the order attracted more sisters, first within India and then worldwide. The membership expanded to accept volunteers within the communities as Co-Workers and Lay Missionaries of Charity. Over the decades, that expansion grew in unchartered waters. The brothers of the of the Missionaries of Charity was founded, followed by the fathers who are now based in Tijuana, Mexico. The order has a detailed website that provides volunteer and membership information.

In the 1980s, Msgr. Esseff began his lifelong bond with the sisters, first by giving retreats in Beirut and Rome, and eventually traveling worldwide as a spiritual mentor. Even today, in his 80s Monsignor is actively involved with the order. He told me that Mother Teresa counseled him to work with priests. Most summers he supervises the spiritual training of seminarians in the United States. He has an astute understanding of the order's history as well of its future.

Esseff: *The Missionaries of Charity have Active and Contemplative Sisters and Active and Contemplative Brothers. This branch of Lay Missionaries has been under the guidance of Father Sebastian in Rome; I have meetings with them once a month. Under Fr. Sebastian's direction, all the various branches and each member of the Missionaries of Charity take vows, including the Co-Workers. We have our meetings, and their activities are really quite beautiful. Mother had this great love for babies whose parents died of AIDS and some of them have adopted those children. Some have gone to work in Haiti with Mother Teresa's sisters there.*

Monsignor once oversaw the Lay Missionaries of Charity for his region, which included New Jersey, Pennsylvania, New York and Connecticut. In the United States alone there are thousands of the volunteers who are known as Lay Missionaries of Charity.

I recalled a visit to Indiana and speaking for a small group of Lay Missionaries of Charity volunteers outside Indianapolis. Based on my observations it seemed to me the women had been greatly influenced by their gatherings with Brother Sebastian in Rome and with the sisters in their region. Whenever I visited the AIDS hospice home in Atlanta, a sense of peace was clearly present in the midst of the pain and suffering. I reflected on Monsignor's words and could visualize that a home in Haiti or anywhere else in the world would be very similar to the homes in Atlanta or Calcutta -- filled with peace and joy.

Monsignor had previously spoken about his spiritual advisor who was the much cel-

ebrated and controversial Padre Pio of Pietrelcina, a Capuchin priest who became famous for bearing the stigmata. Pope John Paul II canonized him in 2002. As I changed tapes, "Monsignor," as he was called by most people, began to tell me about that initial encounter with Padre Pio in Italy when he was a young priest.

Esseff: In 1959, I went to Rome as a young priest and I wanted to visit Padre Pio, who was stationed in a very remote monastery in San Giovanni Rotunda. He had been banned there by his order. He was drawing so much attention to himself, that some in his order were suspicious of this man. He was constantly under surveillance and observation. Finally his superior silenced him, and he wasn't allowed to preach. The only thing he was allowed to do was to hear confessions and offer Mass. I heard that he had the wounds of our Lord, and every time he offered Mass, they would bleed. Another priest and myself took a Rapido from Rome, went to Naples, and took a bus to this little town. There was a woman who met us there by the name of Mary Pyle.

Monsignor sat down to supper with Mary Pyle, Padre Pio's nephew and another priest. What came next was a vision that Monsignor described as one that only he saw that night.

Esseff: In the middle of dinner, Padre Pio came in and started this big conversation with me. His first statement to me was, "What are you doing here; are you a curiosity seeker?" I said, "No, I really would like to know why you have to have these wounds." I have a faith in Jesus, and I have a faith in the Eucharist so we talked about that. We had a long conversation. When it was over, I said to the people, "Does he often come here?" Mary Pyle said, "We didn't see him, you have received a very special grace, he probably wants to get to know you better."

Esseff: He was bilocating, visiting with me. The priest I was with said, "You know Esseff, this place is really spooky." That's the way he put it but I found it a very spiritual place.

We didn't sleep very long. His Mass was at 3 in the morning so it was pretty chilly even though it was May. We went to the monastery and the place was crowded early in the morning, people waiting for Mass. I walked into the sacristy. In those days, we didn't have concelebrated Mass, so as a priest, I would have to get an altar, and you had to sign up for one. When I was in the sacristy, the door to the monastery opens, and he (Padre Pio) comes in and walks right over to me. Everybody is kneeling down. For the longest time, he stands over me. He is angry looking, just looking at me. His eyes are looking at me; I'm looking at him. I wasn't sure how long it was. My friend said it was about 15 minutes.

Then he went over to his kneeler, made his preparation for Mass and came back to me. He took off his glove, which he always had on his hand, and I could see his wound. He

View of Castelnuovo di Porto, a village outside Rome, 2012

blessed me and he was smiling. I was really amazed, as the blood was coming down. After the Mass, I saw people go up and take cotton and pick up the bloodstains that were on the altar that came from his feet. He was asked if they hurt and he said they weren't ornaments, so he must have had great pain in walking.

Monsignor then described the events which led to Padre Pio becoming his spiritual director, and how this relationship would benefit him in giving spiritual direction.

The story of Monsignor's journey to Italy and his private conversation with Padre Pio fascinated me because of my own mystical encounters on planes and in my dreams. As so many living saints before his time, the gifts of the Holy Spirit can also be sources of jealousy from within the community. Later, Monsignor pointed out instances when jealous co-workers sought to diminish the value of Mother Teresa and her work.

Esseff: They said his wounds were self-induced and made him go to hospitals. He had many extraordinary gifts. He didn't eat solid food for years, except for the Eucharist. They put him in confinement. The poor man was really subjected. That's the darkness and he was subjected to it, not only by the people who wanted to ridicule him, but also by superiors and equals and peers. Here is this man who is so authentic but is still being put to the test. There was all this adulation and honor, but he also had an awful lot of detractors, just like Mother Teresa.

Padre Pio then offered to become Monsignor Esseff's spiritual director. He said it was through this initial connection that some of those gifts were transferred to Monsignor himself. An early lesson was how to proceed in their communications. Clearly, Monsignor couldn't always be in direct contact with Padre Pio.

Esseff: He told me that if I needed his advice to simply send my angel to him and he would assist me with whatever I was dealing with. You see, his great gift was reading souls in confession. Some people say I do too, that I have a capacity to assist people in their struggles, with regard to their struggles of sin or grace. Discernment of spirits is quite a complicated thing. We believe that the Holy Spirit guides us to direct people.

At this point I shared with Monsignor a poignant encounter in my own life that I briefly referenced in my first book. It was a conversation with a man I now refer to as my angel. I have shared a portion of this three-hour plane conversation with limited audiences because of the nature of the topics discussed on that flight. I am now compelled to reveal additional highlights from that auspicious Lufthansa flight in 1995 that took me from Frankfurt to Mumbai.

I was in a great state of desolation when I left Atlanta on that journey to find Mother Teresa, after she told me to "come and see". The call within my heart urged me forward despite the heaviness that invaded my soul. I had battled with depression and anxiety after the death of my husband and was now suffering from serious issues in my new relationship.

Since Ron's death, I had severe insomnia and often went for nights without more than a few hours of sleep. When I finally boarded the flight from Frankfurt, I was so exhausted from lack of sleep that I really thought I was close to a nervous breakdown and clearly came to the razor's edge of a complete collapse.

As the door to the plane was about to close, a well-dressed Indian gentleman walked through—the last passenger on the flight. I sighed in desperation. I had two free seats next to me and knew that he would take one; I was right. We were all buckled in, and this man sat in the third seat. I swore silently to myself.

"It was very hot where you were last week," he announced into thin air. I wasn't sure if he was talking to me. "You had a very rough week," he said. "I had a horrible year," I responded without looking at him. "It could have been yes, it could have been no. Your prayers saved your father," he said. Taken aback, I turned in my seat as the plane continued its upward course into the billowy clouds. My father had suffered with congestive heart failure for over 20 years, but more recently his lungs were filling with extraordinary amounts of fluid, which was putting tremendous pressure on his heart. "Don't worry, your father will be there when you return in six months," he said.

Over the next three or four hours of the ten-hour flight, my plane companion and I engaged in the most extraordinary conversation of my life. I cannot reveal all the details of this conversation for privacy's sake and for my son's benefit. However, based on Monsignor's conversation with Padre Pio, it confirmed that I, too, should share my witness of God's omniscient presence, particularly in those moments of ultimate need. We are not alone; I can testify to that. Even as I write this, I am concerned for my teenage son and his present journey, just as I despair in my own hours of darkness and for those of you who suffer so deeply in your lives. If only my angel was with me always as he was on that flight. How I identify with those of you who are suffering alone in your darkest moment and need the gift of a personal encounter with God. May he come to you in the quietness of your heart, or as he did in my life, seated next to you, maybe on a park bench or in the solitude of the room from where you now call out for help.

If only I could share this witness with my son, who does not believe in angels, and has a distant relationship with God, for now. Perhaps one day, the spirit will move in his heart, so that he will know that my suffering was not an act of vengeance from God, but a way to direct me on the path of humility and surrender. I see a golden spark in his heart and I believe it is in his destiny that it will become inflamed as he grows into maturity.

As I wrote in my first book, **Come and See**, I was very concerned about Ron and his well being in the afterlife. My angel, "Suby", as he called himself, told me not to ever worry about Ron again. He said, "He is free forever more." When I tested Suby on Ron's name he said, "His first name begins with R and his last with C—Ron Campbell. When he uttered Ron's name a sense of relief and pressure dropped off my shoulders and freed a place in my heart.

"Don't worry," Suby continued, "That hole in your heart will soon be filled with the birth of your baby." My mouth opened in complete shock and incomprehension. "No, that will never happen," I insisted.

"Yes, very soon" he said. At this point in our conversation, I completely surrendered to this man's spiritual guidance and knowledge of every aspect of my life. He assured me that the journey I was about to embark on was predestined and that it was my calling. "Never give up, never," he insisted.

Airline attendants hovered around this small Indian man with his perfect English diction and perfectly trimmed silver beard. As a matter of fact, the attendants were drawn to him like a spiritual magnet and kept stopping by our seats.

Suby shared with me some of the secrets of their hearts—but nothing that could be deemed malicious. As he told me a little about one perky blonde flight attendant and described a secret sadness of her heart, I then knew that the face of humanity is often confounded and is a mask for the suffering that lies behind a forced smile. I have never looked at people in the same way again since that flight.

I have also thought daily about this man, who was an angel in disguise, who told me he worked in the fashion business for a company named A to Z. The fashioning of souls is indeed a work of the angels as they help guide us through the tumultuous journey on earth.

Mother Teresa herself always knew that her journey on earth was in preparation for the one in heaven, and she told her sisters that she would be even more available after her death. I share a conversation with one of her first sisters whom I met in Kolkata on another journey in 2007.

After I relayed parts of my encounter with Suby on my flight to Mumbai, Msgr. Esseff had his own thoughts of who this man might have been.

Esseff: *Probably an angel, your guardian angel I would think. I have a great devotion to my angel. It just seemed that he was truthful, a source of light, giving peace. If not your guardian angel, then some particular angel that God sent you.*

Going back to what I wanted to say about your angel, this goes back into the mid-50s, this devotion to the angels. First (Archangel) Michael said to me, "You can't come to me with everything, I'm the chief, go to your Guardian Angel with your problems." Then these Carmelite Nuns told me to ask for my Guardian Angel's name, because in the name of an angel is the character. Besides that, when you know your angel's name, there's a familiarity you have with your angel. We do have, in the Church, the Feast of the Guardian Angels, it's in October, and so I knew that I had a Guardian Angel. I kept asking the angel, "What's your name? Tell me your name!" And my Guardian Angel revealed to me that his name was 'Shriek'.

Esseff: *I concluded my angel is named 'Shriek', because he is a loud shouting angel, yelling, shrieking, that's what I took it to be. I used to call him, "Shriek," and he would do my bidding, that's what angels do, and they're here to serve us. They're like our valets. If we're princes in the kingdom, we have a valet and God gives us one. So I'd ask him to do this or that, maybe deliver messages for me or make sure my sister who is dead received a greeting from me. I had these daily things that I asked my angel to do on my travels or meeting people, I would send my angel before me, like I asked my angel to meet your angel so that our meeting would be protected from the evil one, to keep away all that is evil, to inspire us to tell us what God wants us to do.*

When I went to Lebanon in 1984 I picked up Arabic and 'Shriek,' in Arabic, means 'traveling companion or partner'. So a guy who had a Shriek, had this buddy that was always with him, and that was my angel's name, it was an Arabic name. Ask your angel and you'll probably find out who it is.

Besides being known as a modern mystic Monsignor Esseff's main mission as a priest is to consecrate the world to the Sacred Heart of Jesus. Appointed as an exorcist, Monsignor has been called upon by the Church and by his followers for spiritual direction and to discern the presence of evil.

Esseff: *Yes, I think I can distinguish that spirit from the good spirit, from that person's spirit or from a person that died and the spirit that is a disembodied spirit. What was your first husband's name?*

Schaefer: Ron.

Esseff: *Ron is a spirit now. He is a soul so we a make distinction. He's not an angel. An angel never had a body; Ron needed a body to complete himself. At the resurrection of the body, Ron and his soul will come back together to become a complete human. But right now he is a spirit or a soul. I think I can distinguish those too. The Spirit gives to some prophecy, teachers to some, miraculous powers to others and to some the power to*

Monsignor John Esseff stationed in Lebanon

distinguish spirits.

Schaefer: Do you have any advice for people? How to proceed in a more holy life in this century that is so turbulent?

Esseff: *Yes, we are not going to have the monastic era when people left the world and went to monasteries to become holy; I don't think we're going to have that kind of era ever again and I don't think we're supposed to. Spirituality, like Mother Teresa's, is supposed to be in the world. She was not hidden away in some convent and nor are her sisters. Her contemplatives are going out into the world each day for two hours. Their lives are of prayer and they are intense warriors and intercessors for people. Her sisters all over the world are praying for the salvation of the world, for the cessation of war, for the feeding of the hungry, for the care of people. They're pleading for famine centers and against the evil of abortion. Nonetheless, Mother said, "You must go out and see the people that you're praying for. You must go out for two hours, so you can touch the leper, touch the wound so that when you come back to pray, it will be all the more powerful. What you don't see you won't be able to really pray; you must see the distress and the suffering.*

Schaefer: Are you going to be in Rome for the canonization?

Esseff: I plan to, yes.

Schaefer: Can I go with you?

Esseff: Sure, that would be great. Oh yeah, that would be wonderful.

Monsignor then described his own experience of Mother Teresa's beatification on October 19, 2003 where he was present with a group of pilgrims from Scranton, Pennsylvania.

Esseff: I was hoping our Holy Father would have canonized her right away. When I went to Rome, it was wonderful. It was my jubilee year and Sister Nirmala gave a wonderful presentation with the sisters at Via Casa Lina. They had a great big golden tent. I joked,

"You didn't have to do this for my Golden Jubilee." It was (actually) for the Blessed Sacrament. It was a cold night in Rome, if you recall; it was chilly and a lot of them slept outside but they had this beautiful tent for the Blessed Sacrament. They brought up the picture to have in their Mother House and I blessed it and I talked to the sisters. There were about 500 in Rome including the Contemplatives. Sister Fatima was supposed to bring the chalice up to the Beatification Mass but she broke her ankle while practicing and she said, "Instead of carrying the chalice, I became one. It was so beautiful."

Schaefer: How did you feel the moment when the Pope announced that Mother was now Blessed Mother Teresa?

Esseff: She had this message for me, and for so many others, that she had given everything to the Blessed Mother and that her consecration was totally to Mary. That's what she said to me on that occasion, "John gave everything to Mary." It was at her beatification that I, for the first time in my life, told Mary, "I will give you everything now because if you can do this with her I know that you can do it with me."

Schaefer: Do what?

Esseff: *Total consecration to Jesus. I always wanted to love Jesus on my own, I thought he needed my love, and he does, but a better way of doing it is for Mary to help me. Mother Teresa always gave everything to Mary.*

Schaefer: Do you think that she is going to be one of the top saints?

Esseff: *She is, because she is the lowest of them. You see, we got it all wrong. When I was first ordained, I had all this knowledge when I came out of my education. You know this whole 4.0 kind of people who think they have it all together.*

Monsignor then described an encounter he had with a five-year-old girl on his first mission as a priest. Marilee's mother was suffering from tuberculosis and her father was a severe alcoholic. The girl was raised by her grandmother and regularly attended church. One morning she approached Monsignor and said, "Jesus just told me that He loves you more than he loves me. But I'm not jealous because you love me." Monsignor replied to her, "Why don't you ask Jesus whom He loves most." Marilee returned to the altar and once again prayed to Jesus. This time she said, "He told me He loves the abandoned and the unknown the most." She took Monsignor by the hand and led him to a statue of Mary. There was a sign, which read "The Immaculate Conception." Monsignor answered the little girl. "Mary was conceived immaculately from conception. She was never under sin. So as a result, Satan had no control over conquering Mary, and so that's her title." Marilee listened and said, "That's not what Jesus said to me. He said we are all the body of Christ and Mary is the lowest which is the heel. Because she was the heel and the lowest, she could crush Satan's head."

Esseff: *When Mother was touching Jesus in the poorest of the poor, in the least she really felt that was really Jesus. In fact they put into a Holy Hour: "Divine Praises, Blessed be Jesus in the Poorest of The Poor." Because when you meet the poorest of the poor you really see Christ. He really is there.*

The presence of Jesus is in the lowly so if we want Him in us, which Mother did, she had to become lowly. What everyone saw in her was her spirit of lowliness. "Blessed are the Lowly". She really was and that's how she felt about herself.

Schaefer: But she was also a leader.

I photographed Mother Teresa's foot from my vantage point on the altar of Sacred Heart Church in downtown Atlanta on June 15, 1995

Esseff: Remember what Jesus said to Peter and James. "Who is the first among you let him become the least." That's how Jesus picked his leaders so that they would be the servant of all. It's really a very little understood part of the Gospel and I think it's because of our pride. At the Last Supper in John's Gospel, Jesus said He is about to leave them. He is going to give them this big example. He puts a towel on and washes their feet. He said, "What I have done is to give you an example that you in turn may do this so that they will know that you are my disciples because you are a servant."

The leader isn't somebody who is up there on this big high chair and always being served. In fact, the Holy Father has the title "The Servant of the Servants of God." He really is the Big Mahoff and we do honor Him. I think the Pope really sees it as a crucifying place to be the 'Head of the Spiritual World.' He has to be lowly and The Servant and The Lover of All.

Because of my personal allegiance to the poor, I had not always been as forgiving of wealthy people, and had indeed judged them in many instances. I was also fascinated by the verse in Mathew 19:24 quoting Jesus "Again I tell you, it is easier for a camel to go through the eye of a needle than for someone who is rich to enter the kingdom of God."

70

As Monsignor had told me earlier in our conversation, Mother Teresa was equally kind to the rich and the poor and suggested that we never see ourselves below or above anyone. I asked Monsignor to elaborate on the symbolism and role of wealth in our world.

Esseff: Rich in the Gospel is a sense of power. Money can so easily be used by the evil one. Money gives us power so that in that power we don't need God. When you are really rich and powerful what do you need God for? And yet there is nothing more stupid than a wealthy man. Billy Graham said, "There's no U hauls behind a hearse." What are you going to do with it? It doesn't give you the power to overcome death or illness. The inclination and desire for power, riches and this world's goods and fame are really so fleeting.

As a modern mystic, Monsignor also described Mother Teresa as a mystic and suggested that her roots in Albania and later in India had influenced her inner communion to faith.

Esseff: They have long traditions. There are two ways of approaching God; one is the negative approach. The ascetic approach for people who fast and have a tradition of mortification and detachments from this world. That's more of an eastern way—a detached direction from this world.

Monsignor described the second approach as one that is pursued by studying the teachings and a pursuit of knowledge as a method of arriving to faith.

Esseff: We have great mystics like John of the Cross and Teresa of Avila who are teaching us how to come through the darkness into the light. I am very attracted by Teresa of Avila in this teaching. Many people increase their prayer life. She compares that to growing a spiritual garden; they have a nice garden and they run around all day with their little sprinkler and water their garden. They have nice crops, flowers, and fruits because they are faithful to watering the garden. She calls that the Mansion of Prayer. The one beyond that is when you come into a garden that is not raised by a gardener but you wait for the rain to come; then the rain comes. Teresa of Avila helps us with passivity. It is not so much what I do. It's God's work. When my garden increases in its fruits I know that God did it. Many of us in our accomplishments and deeds feel "I did it"...your accomplishments of good works can be your thinking that you were the one who did it. I pray over you and you get better; I did that. No I didn't, God did that.

Mother Teresa used to say, "I pray I stay out of God's way." She realized she was a conduit for God because she was pure and open. She wasn't clogging it up with her own desires and wishes.

Schaefer: How do you become more kind?

Esseff: That's a gift when the Holy Spirit comes upon us. When God sends us the Holy

Spirit He gives us this light. There are various gifts the Holy Spirit, Knowledge and Understanding. There is one gift that is very beautiful and that is Counsel. The gift of Counsel is prudence. The activity isn't so much what I think I'm going to do to achieve this goal but rather how God enlightens me on the way to do it. Our Lord says don't worry about what you're going to say. The Holy Spirit will inspire you and give you what you need at that time. Don't worry about being in front of a judge and being condemned. You will be inspired and the Holy Spirit will give you all you need to defend yourself.

How many times in the Acts of the Apostles, did Peter and Paul face many difficult situations; released from prison, tormented, abused, and they came through it with this wariness. They were finally killed and gave their lives as witnesses.

Monsignor affirmed Mother Teresa's unwavering faith in God and in her ultimate mission to be one with Jesus. She picked up her cross and followed Jesus through the streets of Kolkata and through hundreds of communities where she was called around the world to open our hearts. She whispered in so many ears, "Listen to Jesus, come follow me."

In this world of ours filled with pain and joy, there are days that I don't think I'm going to make it, but somehow I keep picking up that cross and following the light. I hope one day I will fully recognize that the answer is not in being understood but to understand, as St. Francis said in his prayer for humanity.

Esseff: *"If you follow me, take up your cross; you will suffer." The Beatitudes are very much there. "Blessed are you when they insult you and persecute you and utter every kind of slander against you because of me. Rejoice and be glad your reward is great in heaven." It's because this earth and this world isn't really the end-all and be-all. Mother lived not only for this world; all the things she was doing and the way she was living wouldn't make any sense if there wasn't a world that she was going to be with God in Heaven forever. So that the sufferings and what we go through in time is nothing in comparison to the reward that is waiting for us.*

At the conclusion of our interview, Monsignor discussed the centrality of a contemplative prayer life in the traditions of the Missionaries of Charity. Mother Teresa advised Monsignor to expose the Blessed Sacrament on a daily basis at his Church. Her sisters believe they experience Jesus' presence on a daily basis in the Eucharist. When they go into their Apostolates, either in the slums or in the homes, their suffering is offset by the joy of His presence working within.

In response, Monsignor followed her advice and opened a chapel with perpetual adoration in Our Lady of Abington in Dalton, Pennsylvania. She advised him to spread the word within the American Catholic community. Mother Teresa's most significant discernment for Monsignor was to be a spiritual advisor to seminarians. When I spoke to Monsignor while completing this manuscript, he told me that his schedule is filled to capacity. He still travels worldwide giving retreats for Mother Teresa's sisters. However, as he approaches 85-years-old, he is planning to devote more time to the Seminarians.

"That is what Mother Teresa called me to do," he said.

Conversation with Father Benedict Groeschel

In January 2004, I learned about another priest who worked with Mother Teresa for several decades in an entirely different capacity from Monsignor Esseff. He was named the liaison between the Archdiocese of New York City and the Missionaries of Charity based in the Bronx. Father Groeschel was a celebrity figure, appearing as a host on the enormously popular woldwide Catholic Network (EWTN), founded by Mother Angelica and headquartered in rural Alabama.

It was not long before I appeared as a guest on EWTN to discuss my book. News Director, Raymond Arroyo, interviewed me about my journey with Mother Teresa. Father Groeschel hosted a program which was instrumental in converting many Catholics back

Spending an auspicious day with Father Benedict Groeschel
at the Trinity Retreat House in Larchmont, NY

to the more traditional legacy of practicing the Catholic faith. Within months of first hearing about Father Groeschel, I was able to speak with him in person, and soon I was on my way to New York. I flew to La Guardia airport in August 2004, loaded down with a rental video camera, tripod and microphones. I had been given directions to reach the Trinity Retreat Center in Larchmont, where Fr. Groeschel was recovering from a recent car accident. He had warned me that I would be taking care of him that day since his caretaker, Brother Lawrence,   s would not be present. My taxi pulled into the stately mansion that had been endowed to the Archdiocese of New York, and under the direction of Cardinal Cook in 1974, was turned into the Trinity House as a retreat center for the clergy by Fr. Groeschel. I pulled all my gear out of the taxi and walked up to the imposing front door. A young assistant met me at the entrance and lead me to the bedroom, where I found a very thin Father Groeschel sipping water from a straw.

His eyes twinkled as he beheld this slightly nutty woman, who years earlier had traveled alone to India to find Mother Teresa, and was now traveling again by plane in search of more stories related to the Albanian nun.

He immediately apologized for greeting me from a hospital bed, as he was still recovering from the automobile accident. Despite the long journey, I was elated to be in his presence and immediately began to set up my equipment. I realized it was a rare privilege to be in the private room of a man who was revered around the world for his weekly EWTN program and for his dedicated service to Catholics worldwide.

It was not without enormous effort that this meeting came about. I had tried multiple times to contact him through his entourage of protective secretaries and staff. All calls were screened and rarely answered. I continued to pester his office to no avail until one day I was walking my dog Tina in Blackburn Park, located around the corner from my house in Atlanta, Georgia. My cell phone began to ring and I managed to grab a stronger hold on the leash as I gingerly held the cell phone to my ear. The caller asked "Linda Schaefer?" "Yes," I responded. "This is Benedict Groeschel. I understand you want to speak to me about Mother Teresa."

Fr. Groeschel spoke to me about his near fatal car accident, and then, almost in the same breath, invited me to the Trinity House Retreat Center in New York, where he worked as the founder and spiritual director of the Franciscan Friars of the Renewal. While I had him on the phone, I pressed him to commit to a date for me to make the trip to New York.

During those ten minutes of a park conversation with Fr. Groeschel, I knew without a doubt that this was a continued calling; Mother Teresa was giving me the green light to move forward and continue my efforts to document her charitable endeavors.

I recall slipping the phone back into my pocket and silently thanking Mother Teresa for this opportunity to meet another close friend. She was slowly revealing more about herself through Fr. Groeschel and those she walked side by side with on the mission to bring dignity to the slums of the world.

It was not for the purpose of conveying to the world how great she was, but in reality how little she viewed herself. She would show me time and time again, that her work was not to glorify herself but to glorify the one who guided her.

In retrospect, my research on a second book about Mother Teresa began the moment the first book was published. Even though I didn't have a strong desire to delve into these uncharted waters again, I found myself being guided in that direction anyway. I felt her urgent spirit leading me to people who had worked with the Missionaries of Charity during those pivotal years when she was creating an unprecedented order that would spread globally.

Over the next nine years, I was led to many who had walked and talked with her—priests, nuns, missionaries, doctors, and volunteers who had lived in the presence of perhaps the greatest living saint who walked the earth during our time. These were the people Mother Teresa encouraged me to seek out and question, I felt. She called me from her place of rest to continue the task at hand; she was clearly carving out another path for me. "Oh Mother," I would plead from time to time, "I don't have the energy to encounter you again."

To experience Mother Teresa's enigmatic personality and drive was hard enough while she was living. I had gained recognition through my arduous efforts and Mother Teresa's response; but to do this again would take another act of courage. From those I interviewed for this second journey, the feedback was similar. They had all experienced their own "tests" from being with the great Mother Teresa; Fr. Groeschel's story would be similar, yet exceptional.

Through the pages of my interview with Fr. Benedict Groeschel, I hope to reveal the uniqueness of this amazing man's spirit and his exceptional devotion to God, to Mother Teresa and to the world. I have not tried to contact him since his retirement, but I certainly hope he will appreciate my efforts derived from our four hours of conversation on a wintery New York day. We talked ostensibly about Mother Teresa, but during that time so much more was revealed. This is all part of the story of a man who became a priest and for 33 years had a connection with an authentic, holy person. Her name was Mother Teresa.

Priests, brothers and sisters who shun public adulation often do everything in their power to push away the reporters and photographers who seek to document their work. Not only are they averse to the publicity, they will unhesitatingly slam the door in your face if they see fit. That happened to me only recently in Tijuana, Mexico. But that is another story, for another day. For now, these pages are dedicated to a videotaped conversation that I recorded in its entirety and only now present as a detailed transcription. I have not included the entire conversation. I have tried to keep it as close as possible to its orignal format.

Father Groeschel and Linda Schaefer

Groeschel: My dad worked for the Port Authority and built the link of the Holland Tunnel under the river and then worked for Turner as the war began. He worked for them all his life; he was chief engineer on Madison Square Garden, Lincoln Center, the UN and a lot of other places.

Schaefer: Wow.

Groeschel: Also, Chase Manhattan Bank. In his hometown Jersey City way, he used to say, "I wish the whole damn place would fall down."

Schaefer: Why is that?

Groeschel: He thought New York City was crazy; which of course is a defensible position. You don't live in New York City so you don't know.

Schaefer: I used to. I went to NYU and got my graduate degree there in journalism.

Groeschel: That's in a crazy neighborhood. I went to Columbia.

Schaefer: You did. Well, you are a prolific writer.

Groeschel: I don't know how prolific.

Schaefer: I am going to stand back here since I am a one-man band (referring to my combination as journalist and cameraman). Are you comfortable?

Groeschel: I might just put my legs back here a little bit if that will not throw your cameras off.

Schaefer: No.

Groeschel: Okay, if that's okay. I have serious problems with edema because I have a serious heart condition.

Schaefer: Do you have congestive heart failure?

Groeschel: No, I have what is called an irregular heartbeat, which is really atrial fibrillation. I also have cancer, which at present is under control and in remission, heart trouble, I am a medical miracle.

Schaefer: It sounds like it.

Groeschel: I shouldn't be alive. They wanted me to do something before I left.

Schaefer: So, Fr. Benedict, what happened that day in Florida?

Groeschel: Well, I had left here on Friday and gone to California to give a day retreat. I came back on an early flight Sunday morning so I was probably tired and I was trying to cross this busy highway which goes through a populated area right where you rent cars. Fr. Lynch and Dave Burns were with me and they were getting the car and I went to get them some Burritos for supper; they hadn't had any supper and I tried to cross the highway and there was a bus stop and I walked in front of the bus and a car was diagonally behind the bus. He didn't see me and I didn't see him that night.

I had no blood pressure; no heartbeat, no pulse and the doctors finally gave up at the trauma center. They gave up; they took off the gloves. They had drafted Fr. Lynch to suction me. "Go back!" he cried out, go back, and don't give up!" So they did, out of deference to him, and you know they got a heartbeat, and a few days later (of course I was still unconscious) my body blew up like a porpoise and they opened me up. They couldn't find the source so they told the friars to make arrangements for my funeral and got my sister's permission. Which they started to do.

Schaefer: You mean when your body started blowing up?

Groeschel: Blowing up

Schaefer: From the edema

Groeschel: No, from toxins

Schaefer: In the liver?

Groeschel: They don't know where. And Father Lynch prayed all night over me invoking the holy name of Jesus and the next morning the toxins drained and the doctors said to him whatever you are doing don't stop, don't stop. I'm going to have to ask you a favor.

Schaefer: Sounds like there were a lot of people praying for you.

Groeschel: There were immense numbers of people…50,000 emails, and as a result of being on EWTN and the two days after my accident, the Friar's website got 700,000 hits. We have a little website for our community.

Schaefer: I know this might be silly coming from a person like me, but do you feel like God intended for you to live longer?

Groeschel: Oh sure...Jesus says *"Not a sparrow falls to earth that the heavenly Father does not know it; the hairs in your head are numbered."* So, I don't say that God caused the accident, of course not. God doesn't do bad, he does good. And he keeps that evil from becoming the worst. I would have been perfectly satisfied to go. I'm an old man, and I have done...

Schaefer: You're not that old.

Groeschel: 71, I've done a lot of things, but he sent me back. I also had a heart attack right after; I shouldn't be here. The doctors call it a miracle, but it isn't a theological miracle. Because a theological miracle is a complete instantaneous cure. But it is a gigantic medical improbability.

Schaefer: But talking about miracles, Mother Teresa's cause of canonization...are you aware of a second miracle?

Groeschel: No, I haven't heard. The sisters would have probably told me if there was one. But they haven't told me.

Schaefer: The sisters in Atlanta told me about a boy in San Diego who had a miraculous healing.

Groeschel: That may be very well be. I don't see the sisters so often right now; I'm a little out of touch.

Schaefer: (soft laughter) I wonder why.

Groeschel: Can't imagine.

Schaefer: Father Benedict can you tell me a little bit about your life growing up in Jersey and what led you to become a priest?

Groeschel: I knew when I was seven that I was supposed to be a priest and I never changed my mind. I had a wonderful holy nun who taught me. She loved the poor and she went out every day and cared for an old woman. At that time I had seen one movie and there was no no television of course. It was **Snow White and the Seven Dwarfs** on a first run and if you remember that movie there is a wicked witch.

One day I followed the sister as she went into a tenement; she used to bring supper on a tray or in a box to the lady and I went up the back stairs and looked in the window and right in front of me was the wicked witch, this old woman with hair hanging down! I was so scared that I jumped off the milk box down the stairs and up into the church. I knelt there praying right in front of statue of the Blessed Mother. I said to myself, "How come the witch doesn't hurt Sister Teresa?" And something said to me, "Because she is kind to her." So I said to myself, " If people were kinder to witches maybe they wouldn't be so bad." And some voice said,"Be a priest".

Schaefer: From that moment you knew?

Groeschel: *I have never thought about being anything else. I wasn't thrilled about it because the priest lived in an ugly house and had a crabby old lady who was a housekeeper and I thought she was his wife. I didn't know beans. I was a little kid and I never thought about being anything else. And when I was thirteen I read the great poem by Longfellow 'The Legend Beautiful' about the monk who was taking care of the poor and a vision of Christ appears to him in his room and he is kneeling there speaking to Christ, when suddenly from his belfry the bell began pealing, summoning him to feed the poor, all the beggars of the street. And so the poem goes on and finally something says to him, 'Do thy duty' and he takes care of the poor and the vision remains.*
(Father Groeschel recites poem in its entirety)

81

The Theologian's Tale: The Legend Beautiful

"Hadst thou stayed, I must have fled!"
That is what the Vision said.
In his chamber all alone,
Kneeling on the floor of stone,
Prayed the Monk in deep contrition
For his sins of indecision,
Prayed for greater self-denial
In temptation and in trial;
It was noonday by the dial,
And the Monk was all alone.
Suddenly, as if it lightened,
An unwonted splendor brightened
All within him and without him
In that narrow cell of stone;
And he saw the Blessed Vision
Of our Lord, with light Elysian
Like a vesture wrapped about him,
Like a garment round him thrown.

Not as crucified and slain,
Not in agonies of pain,
Not with bleeding hands and feet,
Did the Monk his Master see;
But as in the village street,
In the house or harvest-field,
Halt and lame and blind he healed,
When he walked in Galilee...

Groeschel: So I decided I was called to be a monk of an order that took care of the poor. And when I was 17 I joined the Capuchins. I was a novice in the monastery with the venerable servant of God, Father Solanus Casey, who is soon to be beatified. He was a miracle worker, a humble holy soul. If you asked me who was the holiest person, I knew I couldn't tell you between Father Solanus and Mother Teresa. I joined the Capuchins and I was one for 35 years. For 14 years I had a wonderful job. I was chaplain of the psychiatric treatment center for disturbed and delinquent boys at Children's Village. I will be saying Mass there tomorrow, and the friars still take care of it although there are far fewer Catholics than there used to be.

Schaefer: I love your poem by Longfellow

Groeschel: *'The Legend Beautiful'*

Schaefer: So you went to Columbia as well.

Groeschel: *When I was ordained I started to study counseling at Lona College here and I got a Masters' and the Christian brothers suggested that I go on to get a doctorate so I could teach in the seminary. I have been teaching counseling in the seminary since 1965. I had been at the Children's Village for 14 years and was supremely happy. Then Cardinal Cook asked me to take this old house here and make it into a retreat house for priests. We did and it has been here 30 years. I am the only person in the community that doesn't live and work with the poor...my luck, you know and I would love to live and work with the poor, and I've asked to but it isn't to be. When I get to the judgment seat of God and they don't look too pleased with me, I'm gonna say I tried, I gave it a shot, I gave it a try.*

Schaefer: That's part of the rules of your order to live and work?

Groeschel: *Yes to live and work with the poor.*

Schaefer: But you are, you are administering from here.

Groeschel: *Yes, I do work with the poor, not full time, I love the south Bronx, and I love Harlem. I relate to poor people marvelously easily and especially well to black people, but also Hispanic people.*

Schaefer: Why especially to black people?

Groeschel: *Because when I was a little boy I realized that there was something terribly wrong the way black people were treated. I knew that when I was a youngster; I don't know how I knew it. There was a very poor black family that lived not far from us; a large family and I used to hang around and the older people who were suspicious.*

Why is this little white boy hanging around...you know, because of segregation...polite segregation, but northern segregation was still there. I was very fortunate; I knew Martin Luther King and I was much involved with the Civil Rights movement and the Pro-Life movement.

Schaefer: Most people regard you as conservative.

Groeschel: *No, I am a traditional Catholic. Politically we have been driven out of the Democratic Party. We didn't leave the party; the party left us, and I won't vote for anyone who is not Pro-Life or is pro-abortion, under any circumstances. I think it is awful that when you grew up and belonged with a party that was concerned at least officially about*

Homeless in the Bronx, 1982

the welfare of the poor and civil rights, that the party has been co-opted into a lot of causes which I think are destructive to the country and to the fabric of society.

Schaefer: What was your role in the Civil Rights Movement?

Groeschel: *I was very active going to meetings and speaking for the NAACP and doing things like that. I was friend of the family of one of the civil rights workers who was killed in Mississippi...Michael Schwerner. Nate and I went down when they were having the big march in Selma. We went down to Harlem to march since I couldn't get permission to march in Selma.*

Schaefer: For the crossing of the Edmund Pettus Bridge? (Reference to a historical demonstration in Selma, Alabama).

Groeschel: *They had a big event in Harlem that day. We were walking down 125th street and Nate says to me, "Do you think there will be any nuns here today?" I said, you know Nate this isn't exactly what nuns get into. We turned the corner and there were 500 nuns. And if you were a Catholic schoolboy and you ran into the 500 nuns in their old habit, it is enough to make your heart miss a beat. Oh, it was a great day! I think probably the most beautiful thing I was ever involved in, in terms of society was the Civil Rights movement. I wish I could say that about the Pro-Life movement but we haven't succeeded yet. I never went to jail for the Civil Rights movement but I went to jail for the Pro-Life movement.*

Schaefer: Where?

Groeschel: *Here in Westchester County, for saying the rosary here in front of an abortion clinic. I went with one of our brothers and Bishop Lynch.*

Schaefer: Did Mother Teresa ever go to jail?

Civil Rights leader Hosea Williams leads a prayer vigil at the Martin Luther King Jr. Center in Atlanta, Georgia.

Groeschel: I don't know. Demonstrations were not Mother Teresa's style. We should talk about Mother Teresa.

Schaefer: I want to learn a little more about you too.

Groeschel: The word is Schlep.

Schaefer: Schlep?

Groeschel: S.c.h.e.l.p. That's the word: Schlep. I am schlepping through. It is a nice word.

Schaefer: What do you mean schlepping through?

Groeschel: That's how I am making it through life.

Schaefer: It seems like you are not schlepping. It seems like you are influencing a lot of people.

Groeschel: But it's by accident. I'm over in Ireland and I get this phone call from this nun. "I made eight phone calls to get a hold of you." I am sorry but I didn't know you were trying to call me. "I want you on my network." It was Mother Angelica. I've been on EWTN for 20 years.

Schaefer: So, why would this nun contact you?

Groeschel: Mother Angelica?

Schaefer: Yes.

Groeschel: She saw me on television or something I guess.

Schaefer: So she wanted you to appear on EWTN. And what is your main focus on EWTN?

Groeschel: Teaching the Catholic faith and the Christian faith in a way that has a meaning to the people who listen. And I always try to reach beyond that to non-Christian people; I have a lot of non-Christian people, especially Jewish people who watch me.

Schaefer: Why? Priests don't usually influence Jewish people.

Groeschel: Oh, cut it out. Not in New York. We get along very well in New York. I grew *up with Jews in Jersey City. Oh no, we get along very well. Maybe someplace else but not here. There has been a coalition between the Catholic hierarchy and the Jewish leadership in New York for many decades. When Cardinal O'Connor died, there was a Mass for him the night before and a funeral the next day between the two Masses. A hundred leaders of the Jewish community went to St. Patrick's Cathedral and recited Chadahs for Cardinal O'Connor. And Rabbi...what's the name of the chief Rabbi...head of the board of Rabbis...he gets up and says at the end of the prayers, "I'm not here as a Jew, I'm not here a Rabbi, I'm here as a sheep who has lost my Shepherd." What else could you ask? Oh, no we get along well. Of course, Mother Angelica, they like her too. Jewish people like nuns: the old nuns. I was getting on a plane one day and this guy stands up and says, "Father I have seen you on television. I asked him, "Would you mind me asking, are you Jewish?" He was a real old-fashioned New York Jew. "Sure I'm Jewish." "What are you doing watching Catholic television?" "You and the old lady have a Jewish sense of humor!" Well, I told that to her (Mother Angelica); I told it to her on television, "You are an old lady." She thought that was the greatest. We have a lot of fun.*

Schaefer: What is the future of the Catholic faith? In light of everything going on right now with the priests?

Groeschel: *Which changes? There are all sorts of changes.*

(This was an awkward moment because I wanted to ask Father Groeschel about the scandals within the Church without focusing too much attention on the subject)

Groeschel: *What do I think? I think this silly period will be over. I think we are going through a silly period like they did in France before the revolution and that they went through during the Renaissance. I'm afraid that the United States is at the end of the road. As Mother Teresa said so well, no nation can exist, can survive that kills its own children. It is pretty clear. I think the country is sliding into paganism. And I think what will happen is we will come through very stormy weather. And don't worry about the Church. The Church is having a bad time right now because of the scandals. I have been working with people with troubles for years. Part of it is a media event.*

*The other day a principal of a high school in Long Island was indicted and dismissed for sexual activity with a student. It was on page 40 of a paper that goes after the Catholic Church every day. There is a book called the **New Anti-Catholicism** by Phillip Jenkins, a professor at Penn State. He is not a Catholic, he is an ex-Catholic, but he sums it up very well. We are under the gun from the media and other people are going to be under the gun soon.*

*The rabbi's wife lives down the street and she said to me, when they get finished with you, what will they do with us? You know the Jews in New York don't read **The New York***

Times *because it is so anti-Israel.*
They consider it an anti-Jewish
paper. **The New York Times.** *So*
we'll see. I warn our brothers and
sisters, because we love our habit
and we always wear it. Somebody
may rip it off your back some day.
Don't be surprised if you come to
persecution. Today is the feast of a
great Franciscan who died horribly
under the Nazis. St. Maximillian
Kolbe. This is the anniversary of
his death.

Schaefer: It is exactly my sense of
this country is slipping into decay.

Groeschel: *The church is being*
punished for its own purification.

Schaefer: It's also being scapegoated.

Groeschel: *Yes, scapegoated and*
punished. And I have very many
friends who are Bishops because
I have worked with priests these

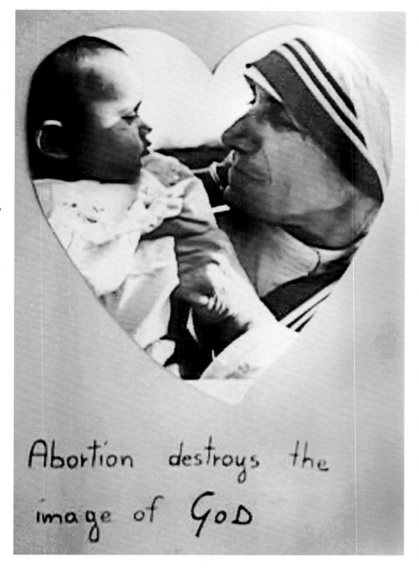

many years. When I write a book, I usually send out 100 copies to Bishops who are
friends of mine and the newer Bishops are very well aware that the church needs reform.
The purpose of our community is to care for the poor, to preach the gospel, and to work
for the reform of the church. That's explicitly our purpose. We are called the Friars of the
Renewal, but it is only because the church does not permit you to use reform in your title.

Renewal is a code word for reform and if you met our young men and young women,
you would be startled by their obvious mental health, robust Catholicism, their sense of
humor, their austerity, and their love for the poor. We just had eight brothers make fi-
nal vows, splendid men, splendid. And they are going against the tide, they got to walk
around New York City in this robe, and it doesn't bother them one little bit, if you see
somebody staring at you in New York when you are wearing a robe...I always say 'are
you folks from out of town?' New Yorkers never stare at anybody. It's not our style. It isn't
the thing to do...to stare at people. Because by staring at them you admit they look differ-
ent, and nobody looks different to a New Yorker. They've seen it all.

Christmas Day Mass at Santa Maria Traspontina Church on
Via della Conciliazione located only yards from St. Peter's Basilica.

Schaefer: Absolutely.

Groeschel: *You folks from out of town? It always throws them off when I say that. You folks from out of town? By the way, where are you from?*

Schaefer: I spent my early twenties here in New York

Groeschel: *In the 60s, 70s?*

Schaefer: Early 80s, late 70s.

Groeschel: *It was horrible then.*

Schaefer: I was documenting the dark side of life. So, I really went through a few years of just documenting the really real dark aspects of life to become immersed in them. I immersed myself in documenting the very fabric of the decay…the beginning of the decay.

Groeschel: *The old monk said it very well: 'After this our exile show to us the blessed* *fruit of thy womb, mourning and weeping in this valley of tears. It's very pertinent. 'Mourning and weeping.' New York City, can be a fascinating place; I love the museums. Once in a while someone takes me to the opera, you know. Somebody gave me some tickets to the Dialogue of Carmelites. But the city is also a stainless steel machine that grinds up human beings and spits out the pieces. One of the things that the friars are associated with is a good council, homes for homeless mothers with babies. We give them a lot of financial support.*

Schaefer: Where did you meet Mother Teresa?

Groeschel: *I was invited by one of her very good friends, Eileen Eagan, who wrote a book about Mother Teresa. Eileen invited me one night to her little apartment in Manhattan. The place was jammed with 60 people. And there was this was this little nun. I had heard about her. She wasn't terribly well known. I looked at her and I said she's so ugly, she's cute. Her face looked like a baseball hit her. I waited my turn and I finally got up to talk to her. And the room disappeared. These little eyes; I was talking to her in an empty field. There was nothing around us. No distractions. We only spoke a little bit. When I got finished I was almost disassociated psychologically, what in the world happened to me? So I made up my mind I would get to know her. When her sisters opened in the south Bronx on the 145th street I was still at Children's Village and I knew a lot of people in that neighborhood.*

Schaefer: What year was this?

Groeschel: *1968. I started hanging around and doing things for the sisters. And she asked me to give them a retreat and all sorts of stuff. And you know she was a remarkable person and a devout person. I didn't know she was going to be a world-class saint, you know, and I knew the sisters and Cardinal Cook made me the liaison between the Missionaries of Charity and the archdiocese. I never failed so magnificently at anything in my life because being the liaison between these two groups was like choreographing swan and hippopotami into a ballet. I failed completely.*

I always tell people I had 285 arguments with Mother Teresa and lost all of them. 'Cause I was supposed to get her to do what the archdiocese wanted. It didn't work. I remember about 28 years ago Cardinal Cook asked me to drive her around to look for an old convent where they could start the Contemplative Sisters. So we drove hither and yon and we found the place. But he wanted her to take over the old Carmelite Convent, which was not the Carob Hilton, I want to tell you and it was in the middle of a very poor neighborhood. But it was a newer building, slightly, just slightly impressive building. It had 60 rooms, concrete, solid concrete but it was a Carmelite Convent. So I take her there and she goes, "Archaw!" (Good heavens in Hindi. "What's the matter?" "It is so fancy the poor people will be afraid to come here." I said, not the New York poor people Mother

Teresa, they go right up into the White House. Well, she wasn't having any of it, so I took her down to see Cardinal Cook who is also proposed for beatification. Cardinal Cook could charm the birds out of the trees. There is Mother Teresa and he is kinda pushing her. Finally, she said, "Your Eminence help me, I am just a poor weak old woman. Don't let me destroy the poverty of my order."

Schaefer: Can you repeat that?

Groeschel: She said to Cardinal Cook, "Your Eminence, help me I am just a poor weak old woman and I don't want to lose the poverty of my order. I would rather go home." I thought to myself well there we are. That's finished. And he got the message too. So, she went downstairs and I stayed behind. He said, Well Benedict, I could have twisted her arm." I said, "You could have? She had you on the floor in a half Nelson!".

So downstairs I go and we are in the car. And she says, "How do you feel about the whole thing?" "Well, Mother to be honest with you I am humiliated but I am not humbled, unfortunately. I wish I was humbled but I am just humiliated." And she said, "Well cheer up, humiliation can be the road to humility." She did have a real sense of humor. It wasn't a rollicking sense of humor. But it was a great sense of humor. I got to know her well. She invited me to go to Kolkata, which I did to give the sisters' retreats.

Mother Teresa finding joy in the work

Schaefer: What year did you first go to Kolkata?

Groeschel: I only went once…I think it was in the 80s. But whenever she would come to New York I usually got to see her. Of course by this time everybody else and myself started to recognize we had a saint on our hands.

Schaefer: What was it: what quality led you to believe that?

Groeschel: Prayerfulness. Absolute charity. She never drew the line. And of course she always seemed to know what to do in a difficult situation, which is the gift of the Holy Spirit. I remember one time she asked me to get something done, and I did, but I didn't do it precisely the way she wanted me to do it, in fact I wouldn't have gotten it done if I did it that way. And she didn't make it too clear

92

what she wanted; she was a little bit annoyed... piously annoyed and I have had saints... canonizable saints annoyed at me, so it's a lot of fun...gobs of fun! So I was driving her back from some place and she was politely giving me the needle. She was always an absolutely polite Victorian lady. She had Victorian manners...Hapsburg manners, I should say because she came from was the Hapsburgs' Austrian-Hungarian Empire.

Schaefer: I have never heard her described this way, that's fascinating!

Groeschel: *In what way? Oh yes, she was a perfect lady. When I say Hapsburgs, the Hapsburgs defined what priority was in their world, as Queen Victoria defined what was right in their world...English manners. And she had those manners. And there I am getting the needle from Mother Teresa; and when you are getting the needle from Mother Teresa, it is like getting harpooned by Captain Ahab. It is not a lot of fun, you know.*

So we got around to 145th street. And I said, "Mother I have to tell you something. I am going to ask Cardinal Cook to please appoint another priest to be the liaison. I can't handle this. I am not angry, I am not annoyed, I am just outclassed. I can't handle this. And she said, "Come in." It is 11:30 at night. And she said, "Sit down". And when Mother Teresa said sit down, let me tell you, you sat down. "Why do you think God chose you to be a priest?" I said, "Mother it is 11:30." "Why do you think God chose you to be a priest?" "I don't know, maybe he had a sense of humor." "God chose you to be a priest because he is very humble. He chooses the weakest, the poorest. the most inadequate instruments."

You know there are very few things that would have helped me that much. She said, "I pray that when I go my place is taken by the most unattractive and ungifted of the sisters, then everybody will know that it was not my work but God's work."

That is a very revealing statement: "It was not my work but God's work". Despite the fact she won the Nobel Prize and these other things, she had no great positive attitude toward herself. As a psychologist, and fortunately I am not a psychologist who particularly believes in psychology, but if you are talking about people who have low self-esteem, forget Mother Teresa. She had no self-esteem; she did not have self-hate. Self-esteem is not something that fitted her. The popular definition of self-esteem was very far from her.

Schaefer: But she had self-confidence.

Groeschel: *No, she had confidence in God. Now that is an interesting thing. When she made up her mind that something was to be done, get out of the way because it was going to be done come hell or high water. And it would be done; and that was it. But it was not self-confidence. I asked her when she won the Nobel Prize what do you think about what has happened to you? We were walking in the streets of the Bronx. And she said it was in-*

Missionary of Charity home in the Bronx, New York highlighted by a mural of a postage stamp released in her honor.

conceivable; it is inconceivable. She did not have self-esteem. I do not know whether you know about the revelations in her letters to her spiritual directors?

Schaefer: Yes I've read them.

Groeschel: *The ones from the Indian article.*

Schaefer: Yes and the letters from Father Brian.

Groeschel: *I didn't see the ones Brian has. Brian is my old student. I taught him counseling. I didn't see those, but those letters are filled with darkness, and that darkness, -- if you study these things,-- is the dark night of the soul; that is exactly what it is, and it goes on for 40 years. As far as I can tell, I know of only one other saint who was in the dark night for 40 years... St. John of the Cross, who wrote about it, never said it went on for 40 years, John of the Cross wrote beautiful, inspiring, elevating things.*

When I read them, I said now I understand something, because there was always a seriousness about her, always a somberness. Even when she laughed, which wasn't very often, there was always something somber; when she smiled, she didn't laugh. The night, the last day I saw her was the day before she went back to India to die. I went down to see her with Fr. Andrew, who is a priest of our community and we said Mass for her.

Schaefer: Where was this?

Groeschel: *It was at the Contemplative Sisters: 168th at Union Avenue. We had an agreement at least with the American girls that were coming in, that they should be psychologically evaluated, and I do that for a living.*

Schaefer: The novices?

Groeschel: *I've done probably 1,900 psychological evaluations for religious life in the priesthood. I'm afraid I might have the world's record because most psychologists don't like to do a whole lot of evaluations. It's the scut work of psychology. But, I've got to do one this week for our community and you know, it's the MMPI, Rorschach, GAT. I thought they were getting some disturbed girls, which they were, and that means you have to put up with them for a while and then send them home. So the purpose of psychological testing is to save the person the embarrassment and pain of being sent home; create a little peace in the convent.*

But she wouldn't listen to me; she never listened to me. She didn't understand psychology at all. Okay, I was willing to do it and Terry Cook was hoping that I would, because he had a few sisters (that) are disturbed people. Now she liked to believe that all these things could be healed by grace, which is an old-fashioned way of thinking. It wasn't true.

Groeschel: *One day I got a call -- I got a call to go down, it was an emergency and I went down and when I walked in the convent I could hear this high falsetto screeching voice..and the sisters were all downstairs. Mother Teresa's sister is screaming at her. They've been going on for at least an hour, so I came down and there was the woman sitting in a chair. She wasn't a girl either; she was at least in her 30s and Mother Teresa was standing about eight feet away from her, standing and bent over in her usual posture and this woman was castigating Mother Teresa. She never even stopped for breath, cursing, screaming, and yelling.*

Now being a reasonably well-trained psychologist I would have tried to put some borders around this, some walls to get the woman kinda calmed down, put the toothpaste back in the tube for the woman's own sake. But, I'm watching Mother and she is just taking it. Well, the predictable, the easily predictable, of course, happened. The woman started to run out of steam and she began to cry almost hysterically and to weep and she was crying, and she ended up in Mother's arms and you know now it wasn't bad psychology. I admitted that brought the thing to an end. Mother Teresa, who was going to India the next day had asked the woman to join her.

Thank God, she didn't do that and the girl had to go home. She was a troubled soul. Well, that was an example, the clash of experiences and values you know and when you are running an archdiocese you try to get everybody marching to the same tune, even as they are marching off the cliff. Well, Mother Teresa was so generous you know and the MC's (Missionaries of Charity) operate independently of everything else around. You don't invite them down to the diocese and congress on religious life or somethin. If you're smart.

Schaefer: Why not?

Groeschel: *Well, because they are operating on different principles and for different reasons. Now since Mother's death, they've been more inclined to listen a bit, but for instance I would love to give them tape recorders so you could send them a sermon rather than flying off to Washington. They agree with me but they won't do it because Mother didn't want anything that spun, wheeled, whistled or anything else. You know up in Mounte La Verna there is a cave where St. Francis spent the winter. Let me tell you the average polar bear wouldn't make it through winter in that cave. The average polar bear wouldn't be able to handle it.*

So these first class people are as the pope said, "Admirables sed non muses." Admirable but not imitable. The fellow who said he wanted to be just like Jesus, somebody said, "Have yourself crucified and three days later rise from the dead and we will listen to you." I mean, one has to keep a certain amount of common sense and presence of mind with Mother Teresa and her advisors and the ring of sisters who went back for a long time, that she had known a long time that she did discuss things with, who were definitely people who did not see things as she saw them and who weren't afraid to quietly and devoutly disagree with her.

(Reference to conference when Mother Teresa was nearly voted out of the order, according to witnesses) *I was around when that chapter was held and I never heard anything about there being a, you know, a knockdown, drag-out fight. I wonder if perhaps it's a story that gained a little by the telling, you know I mean, it sounds like a great story, but I wonder if it really happened because I have never been among the MC's and seen anything but the profound respect for our dear Mother. But some of the people left angry you know.*

Schaefer: Mainly because of physical medical issues?

Groeschel: *Well, or other things they thought should have been adjusted that weren't adjusted. We (Friars of Franciscan Renewal) started a new community in 1987 and guys have left us that were angry and have apologized to me years later, they went on.... please don't everybody love me, I'm not the loveable type actually. And people go through their own insanities or their daily functions.*

Greeting Mother Teresa at the Atlanta Hartsfield Airport, June 15, 1995

Schaefer: I went to Rome with a group from North Carolina led by Bishop Curlin whom…

Groeschel: Bill my old buddy

Schaefer: Old buddy?

Groeschel: In his Mass he said first there was Jesus 2,000 years ago, then 1,000 years ago St. Francis, 1,000 years later Mother Teresa. That is sort of a superlative isn't it? Bill Curlin could be given to hyperboles. You have to wait and see. I think she is our prophetess of our time.

Schaefer: Why would you say that?

Groeschel: I think she was directed, substantially directed by the Holy Spirit, to lead the Church to identification with a poor Christ and a love for the poor with a true sincerity and not a lot of theological chitchat. You have to know the kind of "liberal establishment" in the Catholic Church of which I am not a part. I have friends that are, but I am not, they're not too comfortable with Mother Teresa. **The National Catholic Reporter,** *the first article they had about the Missionaries of Charity written by some priest was a sarcastic and mocking article about these sisters that wear dishtowels. I have reminded them of that because I think* **The National Catholic Reporter** *is the third, you know, greatest human disaster since the flood and the fall of Rome.*

Schaefer: But you are calling her a prophetess?

Groeschel: Prophetess.

Schaefer: That's pretty big!

Groeschel: Yes, that is a term. What is a prophetess or prophet? Someone who by divine insight, by the gifts of the Holy Spirit directs the people of God in the way the divine will wishes them to go at a particular time.

Schaefer: It seems as if our world is veering away from the poor.

Groeschel: Yes it is, but this doesn't stop the prophets. You've read the prophets of Israel. Josiah. You remember the Old Testament prophets.

Schaefer: The Old Testament, yes, yes.

Groeschel: They were pretty good at telling people off. We are just reading Amos in the Divine office and let me tell you he leaves no stone unturned. No insult ordered...uttered. Teresa wouldn't be like that. But she was well aware she was submitting a minority report. She was well aware of that. But she didn't get emotionally upset. I never saw Teresa get angry. She gave me the needle a couple of times but she wanted to let me know she didn't like the way I did something. But it wasn't anger. She's not the only canonizable individual I've worked with.

Groeschel: The only person who had no faults or shortcomings was our Lord and our Blessed Mother who lived with Him. They lived with St. Joseph who died young. How would you like to live with two perfect people? I mean I lived with people who thought they were perfect and that was bad enough. I don't expect my saints to be perfect. Not at all. Mother Teresa was the most dedicated, most unusual, most holy person directed by the Holy Spirit, but she wasn't perfect all the time. You can't be if you are a human being. So, I mean the image of a saint being absolutely perfect is a tutti-frutti, cookie-cutter sort of spirituality, makes me sick.

Schaefer: People think they can't live up to somebody like Mother Teresa, they can't do anything because she is so big.

Groeschel: They don't understand her own self-concept of herself. She didn't think of herself at all in that way.

Schaefer: Do you think she understood people when you came up to her? She wasn't a psychologist; my sense was she really understood their hearts.

Photograph of Mother Teresa in the Vatican home

99

Groeschel: But she erred in the directions of being too understanding.

Schaefer: Too understanding?

Groeschel: She forgave their sins and forgot they were sins in the first place. Or you know, she chose to overlook. She was genuinely a penitent person. She felt she failed God in many ways if you read those letters. I can't tell you that I understand what she meant by that spiritual thirst for God. I have never been there. That's 35,000 feet up and I am walking along....

Schaefer: So you feel satiated?

Groeschel: No, I don't feel that. I don't feel satiated. I never would make it through a darkness like that at all. It's not going to happen to me. I felt darkness after this accident the first two months. The first month I don't remember, thank God. The second month I couldn't talk, walk, eat, drink anything. I was on respirators. I had to cling to my belief in the divine will, which I have always preached to people. Hold onto the will of God. And Mother Teresa says we must accept lovingly everything that Jesus permits to come to us. Okay, and do the best you can with that. It's not so easy. I relied on the Holy Spirit very directly. And I said the rosary. I made a rosary retreat. I said it maybe 15 times in one day. Moving my lips because I had no voice because I had a trach.

Schaefer: What is it, everybody has something it seems. Do you feel you might have influenced her as she influenced you?

Groeschel: I never thought I influenced her.

Schaefer: No?

Groeschel: No. I am standing in the canoe waving at the Queen Mary as it comes under the lowest bridge. I don't think I ever influenced her at all.

Schaefer: You were really talking about what defines a saint and I think that is interesting.

Schaefer: I actually interviewed the new Bishop of Scranton, Joe Martino, on the process of canonization and how it changed in the 1980's.

Groeschel: He was the postulator of the cause of Mother Drexel.

Schaefer: Most Catholics don't really know about the process of canonization. I found middle school children knew more than adults. Bishop Martino gave me a wonderful overview of the process.

Groeschel: The trouble with Mother Drexel's cause - I don't know if he told you or not - is another man handled it before, Senor Jim McGrath and before Martino. You have to have witnesses against the person. They couldn't get anyone to be a witness about Mother Drexel. Probably couldn't find anyone to be a witness against Mother Teresa either.

Schaefer: But you said there were some sisters....

Groeschel: Yeah, but whether they were called I don't know.

Schaefer: Who was the British author who wrote about Mother Teresa?

*Groeschel: Christopher Hitchens' book is disgraceful. And when you are going to write about a saint or saintly person for heaven's sake know something about saints and the rhetoric of saints. There is a similarity between his criticism of Mother Teresa, and the criticism of a number of writers. Dag Hammarskjöld and his book **Markings**. Hammarskjold, I think, was arguably the best secretary general of the United Nations that they ever had. Totally dedicated civil servant. Practically the same day that he became secretary general, he went from his intellectual interest in Christianity to a belief in Christ as the Son of God. And he began to read the mystics St. John of the Cross, and other mystical writers... **Imitation of Christ.** After his death, **Markings** was published. It is superbly, fascinating spiritual testimony.*

Schaefer: Of all the experiences you had working with Mother Teresa for 33 years, if **20/20** walked in for the five minute version of Mother Teresa, what is it that made Mother Teresa a saint?

Groeschel: The goal of the Christian spiritual life is the development of the spirit of Christ in an individual. Let this mind be in you, which was in Christ Jesus, says St. Paul. So a person who is growing in a spiritual life is thinking and acting in a more and more

Christ-like way. But that doesn't translate into a mimic of Christ. It's not that. It's not a caricature. It's not a mime. Each one and their own circumstances, their own vocation, their own culture has to become like Christ. He has to live within them. And that's what I recognize in Mother Teresa, and a number of other people I know who are likely to be canonized: Cardinal Cook, Father Solanos, Father Walter Ciszek, Catherine Doherty, and Dorothy Day. All of these people had their own versions of Christ living in them.

And in Mother Teresa's case it was all the more obvious in her love for the poor, her utter and absolute dedication. I think probably by nature Mother Teresa (I heard this was when she was a sister of Loreto) was rather a finicky person and did not like dust and dirt around; she was very careful that everything would be right and I think she overcame that she was kind of a delicate person. I can't speak of Mother Teresa easily without tears coming to my eyes because even though I was in an unusual relationship with her I was trying to keep her in line and the sisters in line with the needs of the archdiocese. I had my own personal devotion to her and it wasn't easy...but it was absolutely proper and earned, because she was, with only one other possible exception, the greatest person I ever knew. That other possible exception is Father Solanos Casey, and shortly behind the two of them was Cardinal Cook, a most humble and dedicated man.

Schaefer: Why would Mother - I have never asked anyone this - why would do you think she would let me take pictures?

Groeschel: *Who knows? She didn't let a lot of people...*

Schaefer: I know.

Groeschel: *Something inside of her told her.*

Schaefer: Maybe she saw how sinful I was and this was an opportunity to overcome my sins by doing work with her, who knows.

Groeschel: *Who knows? I would be afraid to ask.*

Schaefer: Yeah.

Groeschel: *Why did she take an innocent shine to me? Although, it was never obvious. She didn't communicate that she liked you more than anybody else. She appreciated whatever was done. She was a very grateful person. We tried to do things. She was quite capable of giving you a gentle correction. I remember bringing her into a great hall. I brought her into this great hall where everybody was standing and clapping. I had arranged the event and there was a whole lot of priests in line and she turned around and looked at me and said Father, "You must remember that this means nothing." And I didn't*

Shrine of Blessed Mother Teresa of Calcutta
First official shrine in memory of Mother Teresa, Tijuana Mexico

think it meant all that much but I guess I was young and in my early 40s and thought I must be enjoying the crowd or something. I don't know why she said it, but it gave me plenty to think about. And since that time I have been to many important events that were nothing, and I have been to many unimportant events that amounted to something.

Schaefer: Since my experience with Mother Teresa I have never felt like I need to take another picture. I still enjoy it, but it's not who I am any more. I enjoy the storytelling. But it's not this absolutely urgent need. It used to be like my God, the camera and taking pictures and that's what filled me.

Groeschel: *She changed you. But don't we all change? Think of the music you have loved. Do you like music? Think you have music you have loved in your life. Think of the music you listened to when you were 20 or 30, you might not want to listen to it now. We grow. We change. I never thought I would ever tire of Puccini. I'm an emotional slob.*

Schaefer: Some people change and some people don't.

Groeschel: *That's too bad. I don't know why.*

Schaefer: But isn't the darkness a process?

Groeschel: *But it is a process to something. I think she got there. You don't have to keep the process up if you arrive. Right?*

Schaefer: But isn't everyone going through his or her own darkness, in a way?

Groeschel: *Everybody is going through darkness but if they don't choose faith and accept the gift of faith and hope along the way it will just stay darkness. I don't know how God offers them faith and hope, that's not my business. But, you must somehow reach beyond yourself to God. A person has to. They may do it in their own idiosyncratic way. But they have to do it.*

Schaefer: Mother Teresa's appealing to so many people of all faiths. She is, afterall, rather orthodox.

Groeschel: *Because of the way of charity. And she never ever made the gigantic mistake that many religions, including Catholics, make assuming that somebody who was not a member of their religion was not special to God. See, we Catholics we think we are the true church, which I believe we are. But we have this sort of smug idea that all these other people don't mean anything to God. And Mother Teresa never had that idea.*

When she was working with the incurable people that were dying she would say to them, "You're soon going to heaven, would you want to have the little ticket to give to St. Peter so that you can get in?" Of course they would say yes. "Well, I'll give you the ticket." She baptized. She didn't use the word baptize; it is such a big word and they don't know what it means. (Laugh) Oh God help us! Mother Teresa was a person who loved them all. She had a charity without borders. Made no difference to her if you wanted to be a Missionary of Charity...of course you had to be a good Catholic. Even there, the reason her wanting you to be a good Catholic is it was the proper thing, "How can you be a Catholic if you don't believe everything?" Here were the Hindus making Mother Teresa the Mother of India.

Schaefer: A saint. A Hindu saint.

Groeschel: *There is only one father of India, and that's Gandhi. And there is only going to be one Mother of India, Mother Teresa. A country that is two percent Christian. It's incredible. Although some Indians would dispute that. Some Hindus would say that she never did anything to help their country. Of course some people would say anything. Of course and right off the bat she made their country very well known like Gandhi; people know India because of Mother Teresa. She loved India; she always spoke well of India. Always. I remember her walking through the South Bronx with me about 18 years ago when the Bronx was really in horrible condition, broken glasses everywhere, buildings burned down, the city was completely out of control, smoke clouds hung over the city every day. And she says, "You know it's the worst thing I have ever seen." The South Bronx was the worst thing she had ever seen. This is when Dinkins was Mayor and Dinkins had absolutely no control over the city at all.*

Sister Joy from the Contemplative Order holding relic of Mother Teresa

Auction yard Bronx New York City, 2011

Schaefer: She said so many times that spiritually the poorest of the poor were right here in America.

Groeschel: *Oh yes. I know that myself. I've been to India. I could see it. I remember when I was in Delhi and I was walking along and it was raining and a there was a family from the country that had come in looking for work and they had no place to live. They were sitting on the lawn of a government office building perfectly quiet, perfectly composed with coverings on their head, and they were just sitting there with great dignity, with great dignity. Oh no, Calcutta itself is not an unhappy city. Have you been to Calcutta?*

Schaefer: Yes. I was just there.

Groeschel: *It's a lot of fun. They go to bed about 11 o'clock at night and start about 2 o'clock in the morning. Did you stay on lower Circular Road?*

Schaefer: Yes, I stayed in several different places.

Groeschel: *Did you stay with the Thomas family?*

Schaefer: No, I actually just stayed at different hotels, depending on my finances. I ended up at the YWCA. I ended up at the lower Circular hotel across from the Mother. People ask me, "Are you going to that unhappy country with all those poor people?" I say they have taught me more about happiness and joy.

Groeschel: The biggest problem is the food. You've got to be very careful.

Schaefer: And the water.

Groeschel: The water. Sister came in one day and I was managing my own food, I was eating nuts, toast without butter on it, you know careful things like fruits that I peeled myself carefully and Sister came in with an apple that she had pared and washed. I said, Sister if I eat that apple I will be sick for thirteen years.

Schaefer: What was your experience like in Calcutta?

Groeschel: It was great.

Schaefer: How long were you there?

Sister Mary Prema, M.C., Superior General of the Missionaries of Chairity, 1995

107

Groeschel: Just a week. A week's retreat.

Schaefer: Where did you stay?

Groeschel: I stayed with the Thomas family. Mr. Joseph Thomas was the head of the Red Cross in India. They owned a rubber factory so downstairs was this big shop that sold huge chunks of rubber looking like big erasers. They set me up in the office. And in the middle of the night I hear rustle, rustle, rustle, rustle and I put on the light and there was one of the largest rats I had ever seen in my life. He had never seen a priest. So he was terrified and he ran through the rat hole. So I called upstairs. I covered the rat hole. A few minutes later, rustle, rustle, rustle. He came back with his cousins. So, I called upstairs and I said, "Joseph I can't stay down here there are rats" "Well yes Father, of course there are rats". "Well I am not ready to stay with rats." "They won't bother you." "I gotta come upstairs." There were ladies sleeping all over the place because they don't have individual rooms. I say, "Listen I will trade ladies for rats any day of the week." "Ok, so we will put you up in the kitchen."

So I go upstairs into the kitchen and there's a bunch of ladies running around covering themselves up in saris. Put the lights out and rustle, rustle rustle. I gave up. I went to sleep.

Here is a woman from an old-fashioned Slavic society, Albanian. She lived in a very traditional world and to move from that to India was a big step. But Europeans and India protected themselves by living in European enclaves. And the sisters she belonged to were very dedicated, hard-working sisters. But she stepped completely out of it. She went native.

Schaefer: That's a good name for a book. She went native.

Groeschel: She went native. That's what she did. Purposely. The sandals. The sari. Appointments. And the little room. And the one little man she picked up in the streets. I used to look at her and say what an incredible distance this woman has traveled in her life. And the interesting question, if you are interested in the psychology of religion, is why? Now you have a subjective personal conviction why she wanted to love God. But I say why could she do such extraordinary things? How could she do them? Why could she do them? Because there was an inner direction. The Holy Spirit inwardly directed her. I observed from a distance the effects of that inner direction.

Schaefer: But the Holy Spirit directs a lot of people but they're not Mother Teresas.

Groeschel: They weren't asked to be Mother Teresas. That wasn't their vocation. There were literally unknown ladies asked by the Holy Spirit in parishes but they weren't asked to be a world-class saint, but they are perfectly satisfied to do what they do. I pray every day to the un-canonized saints, to the saints that we don't know about. Many of them are not Catholics. I have a little lady that we take care of: Ruby Davis. The name alone is worth a trip. And Ruby comes on the holidays to get her basket of goodies. We give out 1,800 turkeys and all sorts of stuff like that, and Ruby comes in, a little black lady, worked all her life as a servant, she doesn't have any pension, she has social security lives on it in New York City, and she comes for her packet and she is always smiling. I said, "Ruby how come you are always smiling?" "I'm just so grateful to God for all I got." "Well, now what is that?" "I can see, I can hear, I can walk and I can talk and when I'm finished here, I'm going straight up to heaven like a shooting star."

A wise woman. A wise woman, you know, and she belongs to the African Methodist Episcopal Church. If I had my wallet with me, I would show you her picture. Can you give me my wallet there? This person could be, may be, as wise as Mother Teresa, not as great in the estimation of human beings. But who cares about the estimation of human beings anyway. The history of the world would suggest human beings do stupid things anyway. Human beings, they are very funny. Do you ever stop to think about how funny human beings are?

Schaefer: Yes, how silly!

Groeschel: *Oh God, how pretentious!*

Schaefer: I know a lot of Rubys in Atlanta.

Groeschel: And you don't have to be black to be a Ruby, but it helps, 'cause you start more humbly in life. She doesn't have anything to smile about. You don't have to move among the poor, among middle-class, or even upper class people. You can find those patients that have borne their cross and have done the best they could. I have a friend who just died, Bob McCoy. When they made the list in the papers of the organizations that he was on the board of, charitable organizations, there was a whole column right down to the bottom. He was a stockbroker. I said his funeral Mass and at the time his kids all laughed, saying they were less affluent because their parents were so generous. Once we came out of the meeting of the Sisters of Life board at eight in the morning, and I said, "Where are you going Bob?" "I got to go over to Sloan-Kettering to get my chemo treatment." I said, "How are you going?" "I'm going to walk." It was 25 blocks. "What do you mean you're going to walk?" "I wouldn't waste money on a taxi for a trip like that." "I'm going to drive you." You had to argue with him to drive him. Bob died a beautiful death. And on his tombstone was inscribed, "I chose to follow Jesus." This is a man who was a stockbroker. I don't think he ever missed Mass from the time he was in high school. Generous. He wasn't pietistic. Father Nicholas, I'll give them a couple of dollars. Like 10,000 was a couple of dollars. Mother Teresa represents a lot of very good people. She represents them because she was extraordinary but they are more than ordinary people. For someone like Hitchens to undertake to judge and condemn this person frightens me because I don't like to see someone endanger their soul.

Schaefer: Hitchens?

Groeschel: I think he is endangering his soul. I pray for his conversion. I don't like to see people go to hell, you know.

Schaefer: The judging I guess is a very difficult thing to overcome.

Groeschel: Yes, well, if you are praying for the person you are not bitterly judging them. But Jesus was quite capable in telling people where the train stopped and where to get off the train. You know it wasn't a lot of fun dealing with Mother Teresa. But can you imagine if you were dealing with Jesus Christ?

Schaefer: Why wasn't it fun dealing with Mother Teresa?

Groeschel: Because she was directed by an inner vision in her sight that I didn't have. I am trying you know, representing the archdioceses to get her to do things reasonably. Understandably we got an archdiocese that is a complicated piece of equipment and in fact Cardinal O'Connor got hurt because he would set something up for Mother Teresa and she wouldn't use it. She really hurt him. I don't think she had realized that she had hurt him. J. J. (Cardinal O'Connor) was an admiral and he was into doing things in a somewhat grand manner...not with notoriety but with spit and polish... you know the famous

I have photographed many Rubys in New York City and elsewhere

scene where the priest set up the convent for the visitor.... taking out the rugs and taking out the furniture. I did that interview two or three times. I know that one. I've been there.

Schaefer: You said you testified for the cause of canonization.

Groeschel: *For three hours.*

Schaefer: Where?

Groeschel: In New York.

Schaefer: And who interviewed you?

Groeschel: The appointed delegates from Rome...but there were priests of the diocese here appointed from Rome to hear the witnesses and I went into the criticisms of Mother Teresa... probably the most telling criticism was from some former members of the Missions of Charity who said she did not take care of their physical health. Remember, she is a lady from another world, another time. A sister would come in and say, Mother my back has been killing me for three weeks. "Give it to Jesus." Well, sometimes there was something seriously wrong. I can tell you as a psychologist that most people who have lower back syndrome do have a psychosomatic problem.

Schaefer: Like what?

Groeschel: Tension.

Schaefer: Tension?

Groeschel: Tension. So, people get lower back syndrome when they are getting exams. And these things are incurable. Completely. They can't be cured at Lourdes and they can't be cured in Zurich. You can't cure something that doesn't exist. If the lower back syndrome is psychosomatic even the Blessed Mother can't cure it because it's not there.

Schaefer: You might bring more peace in your life.

Groeschel: Well, sure you can do that, but you might do that by offering it up to Jesus. But sometimes these people had something very wrong with them, at least they told me they did. They were very angry and bitter.

Schaefer: So they quit the order?

Groeschel: Yeah. They bore resentments to Mother Teresa. Not very many. But there are a few. I think it was a clash of cultures.

Schaefer: I heard a little bit about the voting in 1985 when they were voting for a new Mother Superior General. It was questionable whether she would continue being Superior General. There was controversy and some of the sisters were very opposed to voting her in for life. I heard that from one of her own sisters, "We don't want that little old lady in any more." She won by just barely over 50 percent.

Profession of Vows ceremonies at St. Mary's Catholic Church in Kolkata was a turning point for the Missionaries of Charity. In less than two years Mother Teresa would die in her beloved city, also marking this as the last time she attended the solemn consecration of her sisters to the order.

Groeschel: I'm sure she was completely indifferent to whether she would win. I know this after that time when they had elections she positively told them she did not want to be re-elected and if she accepted it she accepted because she thought they needed her guidance. Now she and I disagreed on things. For instance, I would get a phone call, "Father could you please give the sisters a conference on patience or something?" "When sister?" "Tomorrow." "Sister, tomorrow? All right. I have a very busy day. Maybe I could fit in two hours some place. Where is it going to be?" thinking it would be in the Bronx. "Washington, D.C."

Stop the plane. There was a clash of cultures. We were in two different spots. And that wasn't just her. That was with all the sisters. They live with a different concept of time and efficiency and things like that. Look I'm a New Yorker. I've been an outsider in my own country all my life. I don't know what we are, we New Yorkers. I think we are the western-most people of Europe. I mean I get to Paris or London or Rome and I feel more much more at home than in Cleveland. It is a different ball of wax. I understand this clash of cultures. I got caught up in it myself. I mean I'm trying to tell her. I told you I lost 285 arguments. I don't like to sit around licking my wounds. Sometimes they were wounds.

I can understand people being mad at Mother Teresa. She always did things because she

113

thought it was the will of God. Was she always right? I doubt it. Nobody is always right. The last person who was always right was crucified. We don't like people who are always right. Can you imagine if you had to deal with Jesus? Jesus could I make a suggestion? There is no place in the Gospel where Jesus says to the apostles, "Hey fellas should we go down to Damascus or Jerusalem?" "We're going to Jerusalem." Period.

You know you get a feeling that you are standing in a canoe next to the Queen Mary as it is steaming in under the Verrazono Bridge. You are outclassed all the time. That may be very good for us. I know with Mother Teresa I was always outclassed. I was playing Tiddlywinks and she was playing ice hockey.

Schaefer: But did you always feel like when you were in her presence that feeling you had the first time like you were alone in a field with her?

Groeschel: *That unique experience was just the first time. I always used to tell people Mother Teresa is going to be in New York next week. It will only take me six weeks to recover. Inevitably she dropped the dime on you. Inevitably whatever was going on you left with some little thought that was not complimentary to you.*

Groeschel: *She was well aware that she was submitting a minority report. Mother Teresa*

A moment of humor with Mother Teresa and her sisters

changed in the last eight weeks. She went from being this rather somber person who was very, very busy to being this person who was absolutely allegro (completely happy). She was so happy.

Schaefer: You never saw her that way?

Groeschel: *Never, remotely. She was a different person. I think the darkness had lifted. I think the thirst was gone.*

The tape ended and Father Groeschel and I went into the dining hall. We sat across from each other as we ate our salmon and salad dinner accompanied with a relaxing glass of red wine. I asked Father Groeschel again about that last day he saw Mother Teresa.

He described her as a sparkling glass of newly opened champagne. The word "allegro", or "extremely happy" stayed in my thoughts that night as I caught my flight back to Atlanta. "Had the darkness really lifted?" I thought as I laid my head on the Delta pillow. A few years later, I asked one of the longtime sisters stationed in Atlanta if Mother Teresa's dark night had lifted before she died. "I think some years before, " she told me.

Journey to Oklahoma

Between 2003 and 2007, I flew across the country countless times, sometimes alone and sometimes with Paul. I never gave the same talk twice, and enjoyed developing new themes and stories for each talk. Venues varied as much as the audiences I met. I spoke for 1,500 people at the Atlanta YMCA prayer breakfast one morning, while speaking for nearly 2,000 members of the largest hospice group in Ohio the following night.

I particularly enjoyed the small church gatherings; loved seeing the excited expressions on people's faces as I described my fleeting face-to-face meetings with Mother Teresa. "What was she like," everyone wanted to know. "She had time for everyone," I would often respond. "She seemed to know exactly what you needed."

In 2007, I uploaded my vita on a college faculty recruiting website. Within a short time, I received a call, again while I was walking my dog Tina in Blackburn Park near my house. This time the caller was a professor from the Communication Department of a regional university in Oklahoma. Dr. Donna Gough asked me if I was available for a teaching position that had suddenly become available due to the departure of a professor. "Yes, I am available," I responded. "Where are you?" I asked. "Ada, Oklahoma," she said with a soft southern drawl. "Oklahoma," I thought to myself. "Never!"

I would never have imagined myself living in Oklahoma, but that is exactly where my son and I drove one hot summer morning, to meet our new future in the dusty center of the United States. My son was worried and insisted he would stay in Atlanta.

Nearly six years later, Ada, Oklahoma is still our home, and I am still on the faculty of East Central University. I recall that first night after a day of interviews on the campus. I was sitting on my Holiday Inn Express brand spanking new bed and I asked Mother Teresa a very simple question, "Am I supposed to be here?" I heard her respond, "I didn't ask for Calcutta." And then I knew... my son and I were destined for Ada, Oklahoma.

Chickasaw Cultural Center in Sulphur, Oklahoma

Journey to India 2007 and my conversation with Sister Tarcisia of the Missionaries of Charity

July 2007 would mark my first year in joining the faculty of East Central University in Ada, Okla. After having spent my entire life traveling the world, living in some of the finest cities in Europe, South America and the United States, I still don't know how I could wind up one hot summer day leading a U-Haul truck in my Jeep Cherokee to a tiny rural town in Oklahoma with my 10-year-old son.

I had accepted a position in the Mass Communication Department at East Central University, and so began a new career as a college teacher in a town that formed a tiny dot on the map of a state. This would indeed be another part of a larger plan that only God could have designed. It could also be considered another step on the ladder of humility and surrender, which has been my fated destiny in life.

But here I was, dragging most of my belongings along the four-hour stretch of 40 West, before it met up with other highways that would lead us toward a two-lane highway into Ada, Oklahoma. I was terrified yet hopeful that this was the right plan for Paul and myself.

Little did I know then that sleepy Ada would become our home for at least the next six years. Within a short time of my arrival and setting up shop in the basement of the old Arts and Science building, I was already planning a trip to India, and using some of the profits of my book sales to support the travels of three students on their personal quest to Mother Teresa's Kolkata, India.

Through my speaking engagements I had heard of a Protestant missionary couple, Mark and Huldah Buntain. Representing the Assembly of God Church, they had traveled by two steamboats to Calcutta (now Kolkata) in the early 1950s. With Mother Teresa's assistance, they founded the first Christian-based hospital in Calcutta.

In 2005, I had the opportunity to interview Huldah Buntain in Salt Lake City, Idaho, where she now resides with her daughter and son-in-law. That interview will be included in another manuscript. We remained in contact, and after I began working at ECU, learned that she would be speaking at a church in Purcell, Oklahoma. I arranged to bring my news reporting class to the church, where we met Buntain after her presentation. Within weeks, I began arranging a summer photography program designed to document the volunteer programs attached to the hospital in Kolkata. Three adventurous ECU

Hulda Buntain addressing members of the Assembly of God Church in Kolkata on the anniversary of her husbands death.

students signed up to accompany me on this new mission.

In June 2007, Luke Cypert, Jarrod Doyal, Blair Waltman and their seasoned teacher, made the long journey to Kolkata, via several airports. By the time we arrived in Netaji Subhas Chandra Bose International Airport, previously known as Dum Dum Airport, located outside the sprawling city of Kolkata, we were beyond exhaustion. Our bodies ached with the after-effects of three flights and long layovers in airports. However, I was pleasantly surprised by the strength and pleasant countenance my students displayed throughout the trip.
We stayed at the hospital in Kolkata that the Buntains constructed in the early 1950's.

Jarrod Doyal, Luke Cypert and Blair Waltman prepare for a multi-media day in Koklata. We traveled by van to an Assembly of God medical relief post outside the city.

My students carried out several photography projects with the goal of assisting the hospital with its communication materials. We went on several trips to outlying rural villages where the hospital had created makeshift medical care facilities within the numerous Assembly of God compounds.

A kindly doctor who had worked at the hospital for over 20 years traveled on Saturdays with several nurses to administer medicines and to treat numerous maladies to the desper-

Photograph by Luke Cypert

ately poor people lined up outside the doorway. The patience of the Indian people has always surprised me. In comparison to our own quick fix and demanding culture, I have found that the inherent peacefulness within this country of a billion people, a quality that I would like to absorb into my own impatient nature.

We photographed dozens of women and children sitting cross-legged on the sandy ground, many groaning in pain from the digestive maladies caused by the effects of dysentery,

parasites and starvation. The urgent medical issues are too countless to list. I saw women with angry boils erupting on faces, old bandages wrapped around infected sores. The compassionate doctor took his time with each patient and soothed their fears with his soft voice as he gave them free medicine from the pantry.

In the meantime, I hoped to dedicate some personal time to my own quest of documenting the legacy of Mother Teresa.
But that quest didn't seem to go anywhere until that last 48 hours of our trip….

I was awakened at about 3 a.m. in the morning with a profound sense of joy; that familiar feeling surrounded me and I was in the divine aura of mystical peace again. At that moment, I knew she was with me; it was absolutely clear Mother Teresa was present in hospital where we were staying.

"You haven't left me, Mother," I called out

Photo by Jarrod Doyal

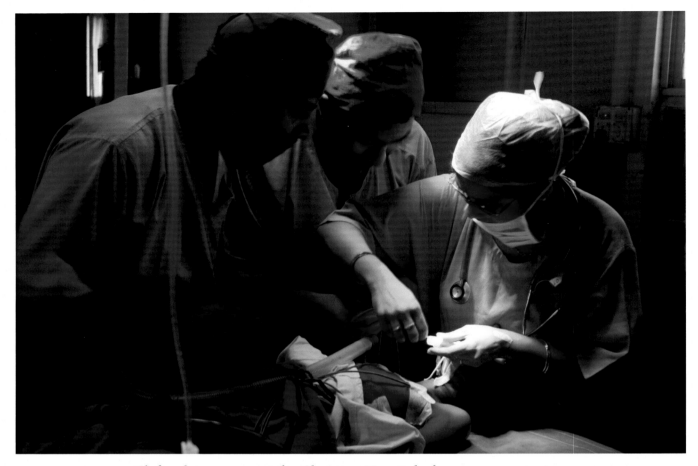
Cleft palate surgery at the Christian Hospital where we were staying.
Photo by Blair Waltman

from my narrow cot. I jumped out of the bed and paced around the room bathing in the energy flowing through my room. I knelt on the ground and gave thanks for this delightful gift of the Holy Spirit. Overcome with blissful emotion, I could not stop chuckling as I had on that day so long ago when Mother Teresa first touched me at the Atlanta Hartsfield Airport.

"You are here, you are here. Thank you, thank you," I called out. If this was going to be my singular Mother Teresa experience in 2007, I would be able to say my personal quest on that journey had been fulfilled. But clearly, the main purpose of this journey was to take three Oklahoma students on a photography adventure to India, and to help open their eyes to the world.

But, I was wrong again. A swami I had met in India on another trip used to speak of the "Leelas of the Lord." Essentially he described the world as a stage, the people as the performers. It is our job to play our parts well; however the play changes throughout our lives. I had learned long ago, the Lord's mystical stage could be so engaging if only the participants are willing to play their parts with all their skill. When the curtains go down, are we ready for Broadway?

Within days, my students were well adapted to life in Kolkata, and each had a daily routine. Jarrod enjoyed his daily Chai from a street vendor across the street from the hospital. Luke was on Facebook whenever possible with his girlfriend back in Ada, but clearly benefited from every moment spent shooting video and still images on the streets of Kolkata, or within the operating room of the hospital. Blaire fit right into the maze of volunteers at Mother Teresa's home for the dying, and appeared to enjoy washing clothes and serving tea to the patients.

So, it was without any sense of guilt that I decided to spend the last 48 hours on my own quest. After that visit in the wee hours of the morning, I was very much at peace as I walked into the Catholic bookstore next to the Mother House on AJC Road. My intention was to attend the hour of adoration at 6 p.m.

That never happened. Instead, as I was searching through the rosaries lining the glass counter in the very dusty shop, an elderly man began to speak to me. We exchanged some pleasantries. He had a clipped British accent, typical of well-to-do Indians who had attended British schools or were educated in private Catholic schools throughout India.

I told him the purpose of my trip and that I was now purchasing some rosaries as gifts for friends back home. He pointed out a teenage boy on the other side of the store, "That is my grandson; his mother is a doctor and helps treat many of Mother Teresa's sisters." "Really," I said.

In moments, I was introduced to the well-mannered young man. I asked him if I could meet his mother. He immediately pulled out a cell phone, and called his mother who at that moment was still working at the nearby clinic. "Yes, she can see you now," I was told.

"Another Leela," I thought to myself as I realized I was on yet another mission. The three of us jumped into a taxi and drove the short distance to the clinic of Dr. Mary De'Cruz.

When I walked into the clinic's waiting room, I could never have imagined the scene I was about to witness. It was a miracle, a sight so cleverly designed for my benefit. I was certain this encounter was another bead on the rosary chain of my journey of Mother Teresa experiences.

The waiting room was filled to capacity with a sea of blue and white saris; at least 15 Missionary of Charity sisters waiting to see the doctor. I was so startled by this scene I couldn't hide my pleasure or immediate need to begin chatting with the women. They seemed to be expecting me, because very quickly we were engaged in a conversation.

Before traveling to India on this trip, I had silently asked Mother Teresa to have the ben-

efit of getting to know her sisters. I had spoken to many priests, but was only able to have brief conversations with the hard working nuns, first in Atlanta in 1990, and then when I worked as a volunteer at the homes in India in 1995.

The sisters were not encouraged to speak to the press or to share their personal lives with people in general. One sister I met in San Diego, Ca., Sister Joy, was asked to write her memoirs, but these writings were kept private and only available to the members of the order. Therefore, it was rare to have a glimpse into the personal lives of the men and women who chose this unique life with the order Mother Teresa founded in 1950.

But in the crowded waiting room of a doctor devoted to the Missionary of Charity sisters, I was greeted with smiles of welcome and an eagerness to share themselves with me. As exhausted as I was at that moment, I knew that this was a fleeting opportunity that I could not miss.

I sat between two elderly Indian sisters; one who was rather round and jovial, the other more serious and frail. I quickly told the sisters about my "Come and See" publication and my quest to document more witnesses and accounts of those who knew Mother

Teresa best.

Within moments I was introduced to at least five of the first sisters to join the order in the early 1950s. I was shocked and couldn't believe this good fortune; I was sitting in the same room with Mother's earliest devotees... those who followed her into the slums of Kolkata to join efforts. I couldn't write fast enough as the sisters' normally quiet demeanor changed into a chatty chorus of voices, excited by the opportunity to exchange and share some of their amazing stories from decades ago when they first met Mother Teresa. I veered towards the frail nun, Sister Tarcisia. She called herself Number 18. Puzzled, I said, "What does that mean?" She laughed and said the first 20 sisters to join the order had given themselves the title of the number in which they joined the order.

There were several other sisters whose names I am afraid I might have incorrectly spelled. There was Sister Dorothy who had been a Regional Superior in New York, Sister Leticia, another one of the early sisters to join the order and then Sister Tarcisia who had also been a student of Mother Teresa at the St. Mary's Catholic School for six years.

"Mother was extremely kind to the little children and very loving to the poor children. She donated gifts to the poor children and on Christmas, all the children received gifts—sweets. She gave a special attention to the exposure of the Holy Eucharist—every Friday the girls were encouraged to stay behind after class for extra prayers from 3p.m. to 4 p.m. We would pray for one hour before going home."

Sister Tarcisia described one young girl who Mother Teresa was particularly fond of, a handicapped girl who couldn't walk. "Mother always brought her to the altar to receive communion and then she would carry her back to her place." Then one day, something else happened, something extraordinary, according to Sister Tarcisia. " One day, she walked by herself to the railing...a miracle took place. Mother said to keep quiet." After Sister Tarcisia had joined the order, she told me she asked Mother Teresa if she had witnessed a miracle. "Mother crossed her lips and said, 'Don't tell anyone.'"

As I looked around the medical clinic waiting room I saw a sea of blue and white crowning the faces of these women who were so devoted to God and to their calling as M.C. sisters, surrendered to a life devoted to Christ.

The sisters were there for various maladies, and waited patiently for their turn with the pleasant doctor. When her son told Doctor De'Cruz that I was in the waiting room, she ushered me in for a quick interview. I had noticed over the years, that in India, appointments are often not necessary and one's personal privacy in the doctor's office is practically non-existent. Most often one or two other patients sit nearby overhearing a prognosis or cries of a person in great pain.

Finding a home off the streets of Kolkata.
These children are part of the legacy Mother Teresa left the world.

In this case, I managed to sit across the desk from the vigorous, young doctor for about 15 minutes. She freely discussed the health conditions of the nuns, and focused mostly on the poor nutrition. She insisted that because of the lack of calcium in their diets, many of the sisters suffered with severe osteoporosis as Mother Teresa herself had for many years.

"I told Mother many times her sisters should be eating yogurt and drinking milk. But no, they eat rice and dal without the yogurt." De'Cruz insistently recommended minor adjustments in their eating habits, which could save many from the afflictions that most of the elderly nuns now suffered. "Mother told them to give it all to God." which was in reference to their physical pain and illnesses. I recalled Father Groeschel echoing that same thought.

De'Cruz had volunteered for the Missionaries of Charity for many years and told me the hospital where my students were now volunteering was not a great asset to the order any longer. She said the hospital had turned into a profit-making institution and was not serving the needs of the poor, but rather catering to patients more capable of paying for medical services.

I questioned her quickly about her time with Mother Teresa. "One day Mother said to me, 'Look after my nuns.'" Dr. De'Cruz has continued to care for them ever since, and was there when Mother died at the home on Lower Circular Road. "I was there the day before Mother died. There was a sea of umbrellas early in the morning; journalists were at the door asking to go upstairs to see Mother. For two days they stayed there."

It was in 1991 when Dr De'Cruz first asked for Mother Teresa's blessings. She would often attend early morning Mass at the Mother House. "One day Mother was very ill and Dr. Woodward was there to treat her." Dr. Woodward is the cardiologist who was with Mother Teresa when she died September 5, 1997.

"Recently, so many sisters come to see me. There are doctors within the order...Sister Shanti for one, but still the sisters don't change their diet. I have treated 50 nuns for osteoporosis; they are all bent over and suffer severe pain when they walk. They don't get it!" she said with frustration in her voice. "It's not worth it."

De'Cruz continued to tell me about the medical conditions and facilities in Kolkata; I sensed the exasperation in her voice as she discussed the growing greed in medical facilities and demands for deposits before admitting patients. "All the hospitals are a business now." However, De'Cruz continues to honor her commitment to Mother Teresa by treating her nuns. "They get strength from Mother's presence in the house where she is buried."

I did not want to interfere with the doctor's work since the waiting room was still filled with patients despite the late hour. I thanked her for her time, hoping to have more time to converse with the sisters. Thankfully, Sister Tarcisia was still patiently waiting her turn with De'Cruz. I sat beside her and asked if I could visit her the following day for a private meeting. "Certainly," she said and invited me to visit the orphanage where she spent most of her days.

I could hardly believe my good fortune as I took that familiar route to Shishu Bhavan near the Mother House where I had spent so many days in 1995 caring for the orphans. As I entered the gate, I heard the sounds of children crying and laughing; the healthy voices of well cared for babies.

I found a sister who guided me to a waiting room where I sat at a large wooden table with a fan spinning overhead. Photographs and prayers were taped to the walls. My favorite saying was handwritten in scrawling ink and peeling off the walls: "God's work has to be done in His own way. And He has His own ways and means of making our work known".

As I sat reading the walls and peering through the door, waiting for Sister Tarcisia, an elderly priest entered the room and sat across from me. I quickly assessed his countenance as someone who had seen the world and served in many missions. When we began speaking, he affirmed my first impression. Father Julian has served for most of his years in Africa. He spoke of his close relationship to Mother Teresa and their shared message of serving the poor.

"I didn't teach. I learned how to live as a human being. The poor are our professors and teach us how to be Christians. The poor are the real professors. They show us how to live and how to get away from useless things."

I enjoyed my short dialogue with Father Julian, but within moments, Sister Tarcisia entered the room, smiling and apologizing for the delay. "Oh no, sister, I am so pleased to be here with you," I said. I asked permission to take notes and she nodded her head. I had decided not to bring my video gear or other recording devices except my still camera.

I pulled out a long pad of Indian paper and a black pen. Page one began with my usual chicken scratch when I am trying to record every word. I tried to keep pace with the three-hour conversation, and managed to record most of it. Just as I have condensed the previous interviews, I haven't included Sr. Tarcisia's entire interview.

Mother Teresa and I believe Sister Tarcisia from the Institute of Religious Life in 1981 (I purchased the negative on Ebay)

Sister Tarcisia and Linda Schaefer June 2007

I looked into the face of this frail nun whose countenance bore the freedom of many years of vigilant prayer and stoic acceptance. I loved staring into her eyes shielded beneath the simple cotton cloth of white and blue. Sister Tarcisia looked at me with an open expression, unconcerned by my relentless questions and desire to know more—more about the lady who began this mission and hovered over it, even now in her death.

Sister Tarcisia is known as Sister #18, or the 18th sister to join the order. It was a privilege and a great gift to spend many hours with one of Mother Teresa's first sisters and former student.

Her presence was so alive and I could see it in the eyes of her sister, right there in Kolkata. A few years later, I would be met with greater resistance for some unknown reason by another sister in Tijuana, but at this moment, I knew Mother Teresa had brought us together. She wanted me to know what it was like in those early years. This was part of our conversation that morning.

Schaefer: Sister, tell me about the day Mother Teresa left the school for good.

Tarcisia: I was a day scholar; one morning for class we saw all the teachers stopping. What happened? A girl said, "Don't you know? Mother Teresa is leaving today. She is going to become a beggar." I asked, how is she going to manage to be a beggar? After some time, the girls began crying. The girls had composed a song for Mother (to do with becoming the school's patron). We gathered in the assembly hall. We were all lined up. We sang a farewell song. We could not continue. The girls burst out crying. I was among them. Mother said, "If you can't find someone to go with you, then go alone with the Lord." We could not continue singing. Mother gave us a farewell speech. Then all the girls went back to the convent. The next day, Mother put on an Indian sari. She put it on so badly. Looking so ugly, she went to the train station—all alone.

Schaefer: Did you ever see Mother outside the convent?

Tarcisia: After three months, we saw Mother on the street. "There, Mother is coming," we called out. We were very happy to see Mother. Mother changed her direction and walked away. She didn't want to see us. It might have been too hard on us.

In 1952, I was 17-years-old. Mother said I should finish school. I wanted to join an order. But when I saw Mother, I couldn't join another congregation. I could not leave her alone to continue the work she is doing. I joined the second group. Mother left in 1947. The first sister to join her was Sister Agnes. Sister Leticia was #8 (who was at the clinic) and I am #18.

Schaefer: When did you decide to become a sister?

Tarcisia: Jesus wanted me to become a sister. I had no choice. Where else would I go? Mother Teresa was my leader. Even now I miss her very much…her love and her affection. She was concerned for each one of us. She was like that for everyone. I felt special with her. She loved everyone deeply at that moment they were with her.

Schaefer: How did the community begin?

Tarcisia: The first house was given on 14 Creek Lane. Mother had no house of her own. Sister Leticia's relative gave that house. It was a full flat. Mother could accommodate 27 of us. Eventually Mother had to find a place to move.

Schaefer: What did you do primarily as a community in the beginning?

Tarcisia: We taught Bengali, English and Hindi in the slum area. In the beginning Mother taught in Motijheel. In 1952, Mother took us to a house to cut the nails of a patient. We had never seen nails like that before. The hair had not been combed in many years. So we *went between teaching and taking care of patients. Before long we found many of our patients on the streets…scattered with bodies…beggars piling up rice from the garbage, one by one. Mother began thinking about a house for the destitute and dying. She approached a corporation. She told me to go to Kalighat…to find a place to worship and to sleep. At that time, everyone in India was unhappy with the situation. People were dying on the road. They don't take care of their people…. dying like animals.*

Schaefer: So how did you get the house?

Tarcisia: *When Mother wanted this house, it was easily allowed (referring to home for dying).*

Schaefer: How did the people in India and elsewhere regard Mother's work?

Tarcisia: *Many people spoke badly about Mother and the work. They criticized the way Mother got patients from the road. They said Mother didn't know how to take care of the sick. Some of the Hindus said that Mother would only try to convert them. Some young boys reported her to the police. The police came and they stood there. Mother was taking care of one of the patients and was unaware of what was happening. The police observed and told the young boys "Go bring mothers, sisters, relatives. They will help take care of the patients." The young boys never appeared again.*

Schaefer: Can you tell me about Mother's relationship to the Church?

Tarcisia: *Mother not only prayed for so many hours, she loved the Church very much. She loved the pope; the bishops and each priest…even the youngest priests. She would leave her cell or work to attend to a priest. She said, "Without priests we can't have Jesus. He brings Jesus in the host." She was deeply in love with the Church and would do whatever she could to serve the pope. The Holy Father used her in places where he wouldn't go. Pope John Paul II requested that she take the neglected children.*

Schaefer: Did she enjoy having visitors?

Tarcisia: *She enjoyed meeting with all the guests. If there was no one waiting to see her, she would say, "What, is no one waiting for me?" It never made any difference what their faith was…Catholic, Muslim, and Hindu. She saw Jesus in all of them. You could feel the great love. That love started from school (she is referring to St. Mary's Catholic School where she taught). It was a well-to-do high caste school. She grew in love with the high-class Bengalis.*

(Here sister speaks about the doctors who began surrounding Mother Teresa as her work grew in Kolkata)

Kalighat, house for the dying, 1995

Tarcisia: *There were many doctors—Dr. Bardan, Dr. Woodward. Mother always asked the doctors, "Take care of my sisters."*

(Donations came in and homes were opened)

Tarcisia: Bishop De Souza told Mother she must open a house with the donation from a lady. He said, "You must take it (the money) and not only take care of the poor but the rich people must witness your work."

Schaefer: Can you tell me about anyone in particular who was wealthy and changed by being a witness to the work?

Tarcisia: Aroup was the son of a police officer. He came into contact with all the educated people. He came from Shanti Niketan (suburb of Kolkata). He was in very close contact with Mother. He was 26 years old. Today he is married and has a small job. This was one of their conversations I heard:

Mother Teresa: Aroup, how did you travel today?
Aroup: I came in a bus.
Mother Teresa: What did you do on the bus?
Aroup: I looked at the people around me.
Mother Teresa: No, you shouldn't do that. You can pray when sitting on the bus. You should travel by train, not bus. You should travel by third class.
Aroup: Why?
Mother Teresa: Then you become poor among the poor. You sit among them and make them happy. Sit among the uneducated. Visit them in their homes.

Schaefer: Can you describe Mother's prayer life?

Tarcisia: We have seen Mother pray. We like to pray as Mother did. During morning prayers, she said very loudly, "When you pray to the Lord, God is attentive to your prayers and the devils run away. Don't pray very loud, but don't keep silent."
She was already a saint. She meant every word of prayer. She would say, "I love you with my whole heart and soul."
(Mother Teresa taught her sisters how to pray.)

Tarcisia: She said we could not understand the meaning of an entire prayer. She told us to take one or two sentences and think about the meaning of those words. Many of our sisters were very young. She would say, "If you pray for 10 minutes, think of one sentence."

Schaefer: Can you describe your first moments of the day?

(This was when the sisters lived in a dormitory-style flat before moving into the Mother House on AJC Road,)

Tarcisia: She would get up at 4:40 a.m. We were sleeping in the same dormitory with

Mother. When the bell rang, we had 20 minutes to get ready. Mother said that was enough time. She would jump out of bed and say, "Praise be the Lord." We all said, "Amen." We started the morning with a short morning prayer and made the sign of the cross. We would dress very quickly, brush our teeth and go to the toilet. Mother was always the first one to go to the chapel. She said, "Let's see if one of you can see Jesus before me." Ten minutes later we went to the refectory for breakfast.

Schaefer: What was next on your schedule?

Tarcisia: *We would wash clothes and do housework. By 8 a.m. we were ready to go out to the people for our apostolate. We would begin with teaching. In 1953, we had 20 sisters. When we shifted to the Mother House, we did not have many volunteers. We had four from St. Mary's School. In 1956 a large group came from Kerala. Then we grew very fast.*

Schaefer: What about your calling as a Sister. Did this satisfy you?

Tarcisia: *There was some doubt. At one time I told Mother that I wanted to join the Carmelites as a junior sister. I said that I needed to speak with a spiritual director. Mother was very worried. She told me, "The priest can come early to see you." Mother was very anxious. She suggested not to go anywhere by temptation. "Sister, I know you from school. You are an active person. You couldn't sit for hours in prayer. Stay active with Mother. Father Lazarus said, "You don't belong to the contemplatives." Mother was*

135

waiting after breakfast. "What did father say?" "He said that I should stay an active M.C." It was a temptation.

(Sister describes her own spiritual calling.)

Tarcisia: *I need to go deep into my retreat. Wherever God uses us. I love to go with the people. I can go for hours to the houses on visits.*

Schaefer: Did you have any sense that Mother was going through that dark period, or as it is called "dark night of the soul?"

Tarcisia: *We came to know of it only when the book was published. We used to see Mother very sad, and at times angry. At other times she would collect us and scold us. I was now 30 and Mother was very depressed. She could not share with any of us. We were too young. Sister Francis Xavier was her age, but they never sat together. Sometimes there were arguments. Mother would keep silent. So she went to Father Xavier and Father Narina. She also saw a Jesuit priest at St. Xavier College—Father Abelo.*

(Sister explained to me that as a result of their youth, Mother Teresa sought many priests for counsel and to help explain the dry period she entered after the Missionaries of Charity order was founded in 1950. The letters she wrote have been published in the book Sister Tarcisia made references to.)

Schaefer: You had a very busy morning.

Tarcisia: *Yes, and then we would come back from our apostolates and we would take our lunch. After lunch, say our prayers.*

Schaefer: What did you have for lunch?

Tarcisia: *Rice, curry, dal, one fruit, one cup of tea, sometimes a second cup.*

Schaefer: And the afternoon?

Tarcisia: *After half-hour of rest, we had tea and a biscuit. We had ten minutes. At 2:30 p.m. we were ready for our afternoon apostolate.*

Schaefer: When I was here in 1995, the hour of adoration was held every evening at 6 p.m. was that the case in the 1950s?

Tarcisia: *Yes. We came back before 6 p.m. in time for adoration before the Blessed Sacrament. At 7 p.m. we had dinner; some dal, watery rice and kidney. We had our night*

prayers for 20 minutes and then baths and bed by 10 p.m.

Schaefer: And now, who takes care of you?

Tarcisia: *I have no complaints. The sisters take care of me. We have so many houses. There is so much love and respect. Mother Teresa sisters are respected more than any others.*

Schaefer: In your history with the Missionaries of Charity, can you tell me a little about your role within the order?

Tarcisia: *I was a superior 14 times. I was a superior in Delhi. We never knew when Mother was coming. The rich ladies would call Mother from there. Sometimes the husbands were not good to them. They were running after other girls. Mother would console them. She would say, "I'm coming on such and such a day."*

(Sister tells me that Mother would fly up to Delhi to console the women and not pay attention to the sisters.)

We would feel so sad. They needed Mother more than us. We would go to the airport to pick up mother. Mother would say, "Go home." She would sit in their (the women's) cars and go to their places to console them. After a short time, she would come back to the convent. One day Mother told us through instruction, "I am not neglecting you. The Holy Father said, 'There are two kinds of love. Give more love to outsiders and second to the sisters. Give first love to the people.' "The Holy Father told Mother the people needed mother more than her sisters. In Delhi she came to see the people. Mother would take lunch with us and pray with us.

(In my next set of notes I couldn't tell whether Sister herself was in Mauritius or whether this was a story passed on by another sister.)

Tarcisia: *I was abroad and Mother told me to go alone with one French speaking teacher. She said, "I will come in two months." She didn't come for one year. So much work was accomplished in one day. When Mother came, she said, "You don't have a grotto here." She was told this was a rented house. "No, you must make a grotto. Call the people. Get cement and stones and make it!" Mother instructed the boys on how to make the grotto. She was very good at making the sisters uncomfortable. By 4:30 p.m. she told us to get all the people. "Now the grotto is complete," she said. "Now let us pray to Our Lady." Then we had tea and put Mother's sari together and started for the airport. She came in the morning and finished all the work by the end of the day. She slept on the journey.*

Celebration around the Grotto inside Mother House in Kolkata

Tarcisia: *In 1980 we managed to get the first group of ladies released from jail. Mother felt that we were not doing enough for the poor women in jail. She asked me to visit the women in prison. I went. I asked for the superintendent. He said,*

138

"Alone, what can you do? Visit some of the ladies? You can't do much." We were told that some of the ladies were not guilty but were not released because they had no place to go. I told Mother. Mother got ready with her Hindu co-workers to release the women. In 1980 about 30 women were released. They had been abandoned for a long time in jail. They had no one to talk to. Some were from Pakistan. I found they had become mental defectives from no hope in life and no communication. Today the Lay Missionaries of Charity are visiting the women and seeing to their needs. We are trying to see to their needs spiritually.

In closing, Sister Tarcisia shared a story from the prison.

One day the prisoners were not permitted to attend the mosque, temple or chapel. One young man fasted and said that Jesus is the true God, and if he weren't allowed to go to the chapel he would fast. The prison guards wouldn't listen; the superintendent became anxious. He asked the Missionaries of Charity sisters to come to the jail; we went to the jail... They called the boy.
(In the end, the superintendent permitted prayer again throughout the prison.)

Tarcisia: *He listened to us and told the boy, "We are sorry this happened." We got up and said, "We are the salt of the world. We are the light of the world. We are the truth." The New Testament brought life to them (in prison). I became happy working in the jail because I learned so much. The boy said he wanted to be baptized. We can live in jail and go to Jesus.*

Sitting with the elderly Missionary of Charity sister at the orphanage, was as if I was seated with Mother Teresa herself; learning about the moment Mother Teresa left the Loretto Order forever to follow the calling she was given by Jesus: to open homes around the world that would serve the poorest of the poor.

Mother Teresa's influence in Kolkata

Mother Teresa became an iconic symbol of compassion for the world through her simple message of doing "small things with great love." She didn't seek fame or wealth. She died on a tiny cot in her beloved convent in the city she adopted as her own.

A young man who visited Mother Teresa on a regular basis understood her message of compassion in action. The very next day after meeting with Sister Tarcisia, I met Paritosh Majumdar at the St. Xavier Catholic College where I also hoped to interview the elderly Father Abelo.

The college is located close to the hospital where we were staying. I walked the few blocks to the school and without an appointment, wandered through the empty hallways. Within minutes, a young man appeared out of nowhere and invited me to have some coffee in the cafeteria.

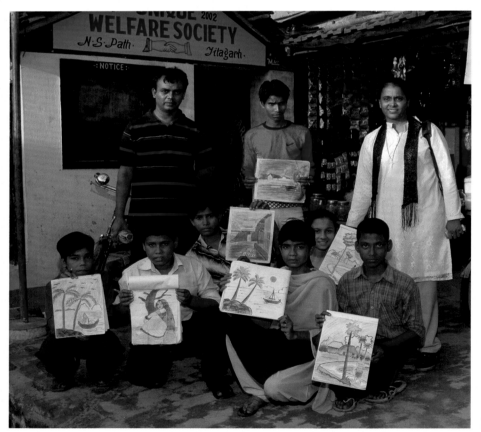

Paritosh posing with a group of students he is assisting in Titigarh

A graduate of the college in business, Paritosh told me that over the past two years, he had been founding and was building a non-profit charitable organization to assist widows and children in the outlying slums of Kolkata. He invited me to travel by taxi to some of the facilities near Titigarh where Mother Teresa's leper colony was also located.

After a quick tour of the college, we jumped into one of the older gigantic yellow taxis and drove the 45-minute ride to Titigarh. I was familiar with the area, since I had visited Gandhi Prem Nivas, the colony Mother Teresa founded in the early 1950s.

We pulled up to one of the sprawling roadside communities and Paritosh led me down a few alleys until we arrived at his simple home. It also served as the headquarters for his homegrown charity. We continued our walking tour of the neighborhood and my new friend led me to a building, buzzing with activity. A dozen women were busy at work knitting sweaters and scarves, which would serve to support their families. Paritosh had learned from Mother Teresa herself how to serve the people of his own community.

Paritosh then told me that he wanted to show me the poorest slum in the area. We took another taxi to an inner community and a compound that I suspect few foreigners like myself had ever set foot in.

The moment we stepped out of the taxi into the hot, humid air, the stench of garbage and open sewers hit me as if a cloak of contaminated air had fallen over me. I was taken aback, first by the horrific smell, and then by the visual sadness of what lay in front of me. I had never encountered such poverty. At that instance, I also recognized that it was this very scene was my main purpose on this trip to India. "She wants me to see what she saw," I said to myself at that moment. We crossed the border from poverty into absolute destitution. That border was an open sewer with steam coming off the stagnant black and

A woman recycling garbage in the midst of her home

Soccer team of the Titigarh slums. Finding joy despite kicking without shoes

green water that killed all the surrounding vegetation, with the exception of a few struggling weeds.

In the center of a circular community, I saw that this was a human garbage dump and that the people were actually living on a trail of recycled garbage. In the middle of the clapboard housing, was a pile of cans, plastic bags and pieces of colorful rags.

A group of partly clothed children came running towards us, smiling at these unexpected visitors. They followed us on our tour. We came upon a group of boys playing soccer. I had to prevent myself from crying. Few of the boys even wore socks to kick the worn out ball. The ragged clothes, torn up shoes and dirty bodies, couldn't prevent these boys from running across the dusty field to score a point. They smiled for my camera and I captured this soccer team with one of my last rolls of color negative film.

The shock of this recognition in my unexpected mission has continued to occupy my thoughts over the years. Whenever I hear about a new slanderous remark regarding Mother Teresa, I think about this slum, and how it must have looked much like the one where Mother Teresa first began her work. She formed a school by drawing in the sand. She loved one person at a time. She did it for the love of God. How many of us can say, we have loved that much?

Journey from the Ganges river in Veranasi, India...

...To the Tiber River in Rome, Italy

Rome, Italy 2012

My city, my Roma, my Italy. Paul and I were flying to Rome for Christmas.

Castelnuovo di Porto, the village Paul and I stayed with my old school friend Chris Warde-Jones

Our arrival date was Christmas Eve at 2:05 p.m. Two weeks before our flight from Dallas, I sent an email to the Bishop's office of the Vatican hoping that Paul and I could attend the Christmas Eve Mass at St. Peter's Basilica. I also left a voice message, hoping for a reply, despite the late request for two tickets. Normally pilgrims and tourists are asked to correspond months in advance of attending Mass with the Holy Father.

To my surprise, the day before our departure, my iPhone rang sharply while I was driving down Main Street, Ada. Sister Christina was on the other end, calling from the Bishop's Office in Rome. She informed me that I indeed had two tickets for the Christmas Eve Mass and would have to pick them up before noon on December 24.

I was thrilled by the unexpected call, but almost immediately frightened by the prospect of not being able to collect the tickets and making it on time for the actual Mass.

I immediately sent an email to my old school friend, Chris Warde-Jones who Paul and I would be meeting on Christmas Day, to see if he could collect the tickets. I also tried to reach a courier service in Rome to no avail.

As Paul and I were driving to Dallas to catch the British Airways flight to Rome, via London, I thought back on that last flight to Rome in 2003. "Rome is always magical for me," I thought. "Is she going to be magical this time?" I reminisced back further to the morning my mother; sister, brother and I flew into the Rome airport when I was only 11-years-old. It was indeed a magical moment when we drove through the streets of Rome that day. "I'm in love, I'm in love with this city," I thought then.

Could it happen a third time? Could that magnetism still exist?

By the time Paul and I arrived at Heathrow Airport in the early morning absolutely worn out, I thought, "There is no way we are going to make the Mass." I sent Chris a text and told him not to make the effort to fetch our tickets. He responded quite quickly with a relieved response since his day was going to be filled with family activities.

On our flight from London to Rome, sadness descended on me.
"Rome might not be magical this time," I thought.

Paul was completely exhausted when we arrived in the Fiumicino Airport. I had managed to drift off to sleep a few times on the cramped flight, but it was clear that we would need some recovery time.

We were greeted at the airport by a taxi service, and taken to our bed and breakfast hotel located on the famous Via dell Conciliazione only yards from the Vatican. Paul and I lugged our bags up an old cranky elevator and into the cramped hotel room. Paul immediately fell onto the narrow extra cot that was drawn close to the window that had a straight view of St. Peter's Basilica. I looked out the window and knew that I had a mission.

Christmas Eve Mass at St. Peter's Basilica

While Paul was sleeping, I jumped into a typically badly engineered Roman shower and washed off the grime from two airplanes and several airports. The water spilled out onto the floor due to an imbalanced shower floor. "Ah well, at least the water is fairly warm," I thought. As I wrapped a white towel my head, I did my usual checklist of what I would need for a tour of St. Peter's Square.

I grabbed a pair of fresh jeans out of my suitcase and bundled up for the cold air. Next, I opened my camera bag and made sure my new Nikon D800e was fully loaded with a new memory card and charged battery. I left my purse in the hotel room, but pulled out my iPhone and some Euros, which I tucked into the bag.

The Swiss Guard who directed me Christmas Eve

Pulling a black hat over my ears, I wrapped a cashmere shawl around my neck and stepped onto Via Della Conciliazione. It was breathtaking. Pilgrims from around the world were already flowing onto St. Peter's Piazza. For a moment, I was pulled by two opposing desires: to do anything in my power to get two tickets for the Christmas Eve Mass, or to simply let it go and make this a pure Roman holiday.

That sense of responsibility, bred into me at early age, won. I quickened my pace and picked up my gait towards the gigantic Basilica with a new goal. I had no idea how this would manifest. I had no tickets, and had been told that it took months to even usually get a response. So, how was I going to acquire two tickets at the last hour? I made the thoughts come to a screeching halt, and instead put myself into high action gear mode. "Anything is possible with God," I reassured myself.

I saw several European tourists speaking to a Swiss Guard at the left entrance to the Vatican. I waited impatiently to speak to the young man dressed in the circus-like outfit that so easily identified these protectors of the papal residence. Finally, the guard's attention was free and I approached him before he could return to his spot the the framed arch to join his companion guard.

I quickly told him my situation with the tickets that had been promised to me, but that because of the timing of my arrival, were still sitting in the Bishop's office. "Go speak to the guards at the bronze door, " he responded curtly.

I had no idea of the location of the bronze door, but ran to the other side of the piazza and asked a police officer for further directions. He pointed towards the massive white columns and another arch where more guards and secret service would be stationed for the night's Mass.

This seemed to be the main guarding post for the Vatican. Once again, I told the guards of my predicament. Several officers and what appeared to be secret service agents, peered at me with mild interest. They had most definitely heard thousands of stories, and had most likely had to respond to unusual requests.

This Swiss Guard opened a thick ledger with the names of all the invited guests for the evening. My name was not on the list. "That's because it is on another list," I insisted. "But I have two reserved chairs for the evening," I continued. "No, without a ticket, you can not come in," was the steadfast response.

My argument seemed futile, but I knew that I was supposed to be in the Basilica that evening and that Paul was supposed to be with me to witness the holy Mass. I continued trying to convince the guards that I needed a special privilege for that evening. "I'm certain that some of those guests on the list will not be here tonight," I argued. "Please give me two tickets." Finally, the guard relented and opened a desk drawer. He pulled out two green tickets and handed them to me. "You should get in line soon if you want to make it into the church." I thanked him profusely and ran to my hotel knowing that I would face an angry son who would not be as inspired as myself to stand in a three-hour line for a Mass after not sleeping for 24 hours.

I was right of course. Paul was furious when I shook him awake. "Hurry Paul, you need to get dressed." "I'm not going, mom," he insisted. "I'm exhausted." "I know Paul, but this is the only thing I'm going to make you do in Rome. Don't wear jeans Paul," I continued as I ran into the bathroom with black pants and a more formal sweater to change out of the jeans.

Paul consented, knowing that his mother would not let him off the hook this time. We stopped at a Panera for a sandwich and drink and then headed towards the already very long line that circled the piazza. We went to the back of the line and for the next three hours were sandwiched between two orders of nuns. Their lack of impatience inspired me with more patience.

As I shivered in my black coat, I noticed one of the young sisters standing in a pair of open sandals. She wrapped a blue scarf around her face and gazed in expectant devotion. She was beautiful and reminded me of a young Mary or Mother Teresa.

Paul and I took turns leaving the line to huddle with other cold tourists on the steps leading up to the church. I also circled the piazza a few times to take photographs of the gathering crowds and glowing light on the ancient cobblestoned ground.

Finally, we saw movement by the entrance to the church. It was close to 8:30 p.m; we had been standing in line since 5 p.m. A new urgency swept through the crowd. The goal was simple: to get into the church, and many of us would never make it up the stairs once St. Peter's filled to capacity. I silently counted the crowd in front and behind us. I thought for sure we would get inside the doors; I was right, but it was close.

The lines began gathering early in the afternoon on Christmas Eve outside St. Peter's Basilica. The glowing light seemed ethereal as it partially lit the thousands of pilgrims gathered for Pope Benedict's last homily of 2012

Ceremonies before the Christmas Eve Mass celebrations

Paul and I were in the last group that actually made it through the tall wooden doors. We quickly rushed to find two chairs close to the back of the church. Dozens of people crammed by the door, behind a barricade. They were pleased to be there even though they had to stand.

The music began and the arches and dome, which seemed to lift the ethereal sounds of the choir to a heavenly level in our limited space, magnified it. I waited expectantly for the Mass to proceed, and wished that we could have been closer to the front.

In the meantime, there was some urgent movement among the well-dressed Italian secret service as they moved towards the barricades. I had no idea that this Mass would be conducted like any other Mass in the Catholic Church. The pastor follows a group of altar server children to the main altar. That is exactly the protocol in St. Peter's. The hallway was being prepared for the entrance of Pope Benedict XVI, and I had a direct view of the door from which he would shortly emerge.

I asked Paul to guard my bag as I followed one of the pope's secret service men to the barricade. He was shorter than me, but held his position firmly. An Italian woman next to me made it almost impossible to hold my camera in a favorable position for when the Pope was driven into public view. I made sure all my camera settings were in place and decided to work without flash. I increased my ISO and my shutter speed. I was ready.

As I waited in the bone-chilling cold outside St. Peter's Basilica, this sister's contemplative gaze caught my attention and the moment was caught through the lens of my camera.

My first view of Pope Benedict XVI as he begins to process down the aisle of St. Peter's Basilica Christmas Eve 2012

The door opened, and an excited cry emerged from the thousands gathered at that moment. First, a dozen cardinals dressed in white walked slowly past us. They were followed by a group of very happy children who would be serving the Holy Father during Mass. Then, for the first time I saw the elderly Pope through my viewfinder, and was surprised by his small stature.

As he drove by our group, I managed to snap a few photographs. Then I rushed to an open chair for a better view of Pope Benedict as he moved up the long aisle of the church. A guard pulled me off the chair. I didn't mind. I had my photograph. Paul and I had seized the moment, and I knew without a doubt that this is where we had been destined to be that night.

At that moment when I first viewed the Holy Father, it was very different than when I first looked into the eyes of Pope John Paul II. I couldn't help but feel that the previous pope had a stronger charisma. In Pope Benedict, I saw an elderly priest who presided over a massive Catholic Church.

Paul and I ate a very late dinner that night. We ate in a small restaurant nearby the Vatican. I thoroughly enjoyed a small bottle of Chianti to accompany my spaghetti with clam sauce. Paul was not impressed with his microwaved pasta dish. "I thought the food would be better in Rome," he commented. It was a glorious night in Rome, and I knew that there was a purpose to our visit.

The next morning, the soft gray light coming through the open portions of the long curtains awakened me. Paul was curled up on a very uncomfortable looking cot, but I knew he would continue to sleep for another two hours at least. It was around 9:00 a.m.

We were staying at St. Peter's Temporary Room bed and breakfast. I decided to have a hurried coffee and bread before checking out Christmas morning in Rome. The buffet table of the small dining room was loaded with fresh rolls and a bountiful supply of cheese and salamis. I enjoyed two cups of strong espresso, and on another mission, prepared for Via Della Conciliazione once again.

Christmas morning in Rome facing St. Peter's Basilica gave me a sense of purposefulness and my love for Rome resurfaced. "I love this city," I thought as I lifted my camera to a new spectacle moving towards me. Dozens of colorfully dressed runners lined the very wide street and were moving towards me. I quickly darted out into the middle of the avenue and took some photographs of the runners with St. Peter's behind them. "Lovely shot," I thought to myself.

After the runners passed me, I saw two nuns struggling to photograph themselves with St.

Peter's in the background. I offered to help much to their relief. I then took some photographs of the middle-aged women with my own camera and we began to have a conversation.

I learned that Sister Laura Combona had only arrived in Rome the day before after living for 28 years in Ethiopia. She was planning to attend Christmas Mass at Santa Maria Traspontina Church. Sister Agnes who was accompanying Sister Laura spoke little English but was content to smile and listen to our conversation.

I told the sisters about my Mother Teresa book and my plans to spend one day touring the Missionary of Charity facilities in Rome.

"The order has changed so much since Mother Teresa died," she lamented. Curious as to her perspective, I let her go on without leading her. "The sisters are very afraid of being taken advantage of. They have become very secretive and reclusive since Mother Teresa's death. They do not want to be misrepresented."

I shared a little bit of my journey with Mother Teresa, and offered to run up to my hotel room for a copy of my book. The sisters were delighted by my gift when I returned with a copy in hand. "They are selling this book in the Sheraton Hotel in my city," Sister Combona informed me. "Really," I said, not surprised at all since it appears *Come and See* is being sold worldwide without my authorization.

Sister Combona continued with her observations. "Mother Teresa might be the last saint in the Catholic Church." "What?" Now I was amazed that on Christmas morning I would be having such a conversation with a woman who had taken her vows nearly three decades ago and whom I had never met until that moment on Via della Conciliazione.

"What do you mean by that?" I asked. "The church is choking. There is no oxygen," she replied with authority. "In order for a saint to emerge in the Church, the Holy Spirit must be free to move and to find someone who is receptive to do the work of God." I let her continue. "The church feels safe right now, but it isn't. It is dying."

I was awestruck. Sister Combona looked at her watch and said it was time for Mass across the street at Santa Maria Traspontina church. I knew Paul would still be asleep so I agreed to accompany the women to church.

This was indeed a perfect moment for me…. to be spending an hour with two lovely nuns who were so open and welcoming of this stranger from the United States. We sat in a pew, and I soaked in the sacred space around us. Thousands had sat on this very bench, gazing up at the glorious painting of the Renaissance in appreciation of the long history of Roman Catholic Church.

Attending Christmas Mass with Sisters Laura and Agnes.

The priest gave a Mass in Italian, which I no longer understood, but I was overjoyed to be experiencing this amazing hour on Christmas morning. I wished Paul could be there with me. The priest made an observation and everyone clapped. "See, this priest is a good man," said Sister Combona. "He is part of the old world. He allows people to clap." She also pointed out the young altar girls. "He allows the girls to be a part of the Mass."

We parted ways on Via Della Conciliazione and promised to stay in touch by email. I gazed for a moment at the majesty of St. Peter's Basilica, and again, appreciated the wonderment of this journey. The last time I viewed the church was at Mother Teresa's beatification, and a photograph of the newly Blessed Teresa of Calcutta gazed back at me. Now, she was no longer present in the Square, but I knew that her spirit would always be available to me through a prayer or a conversation.

Msgr. Esseff said that Mother Teresa's work would live on through her sisters. Paul and I met with Sister Marise Therese M.C. whom I had known in Atlanta, Georgia. We had remained in communication when she was transferred to Rome to work in the archives office.

Two days after Christmas, we joined her at St. Peter's Square and went on a tour of the nativities at the churches, and then a short tour of the home Mother Teresa established at the Vatican under the guidance of Pope John Paul II.

She was overjoyed by the prospect of now being transferred to Kigali, Rwanda to serve as a much-needed nurse at the orphanage established by the order. I gazed, once again into the eyes of compassion that reflected joy in the work and in her service to humanity.

Conclusion

I was squeezed between a guard and a very determined Italian woman, but I managed to brace my Nikon D800e for this moment.

And so I come to end of this latest work, and hope you have learned something new from my journey. I have had many more conversations that I also hope to share with you one day.

As I was completing this manuscript, Pope Benedict XVI resigned and shocked the world. I was thankful to realize that my photograph of the pope would be one of the last taken of him in a public Mass. I recalled my conversation, again with the two sisters on Christmas Day, and it seemed fitting that the Pope would declare 2013 the "Year of Faith".

That faith would be tested once again when the Bishop of Cardinals elected one among them who named himself Pope Francis. I was overjoyed as I was glued to CNN and watched the new pope open his arms to his new flock.

Throughout my life, I had a strong connection to St. Francis and have statuary and photographs of the great saint displayed throughout my house and office. Mother Teresa asked that the prayer of St. Francis be a reminder in homes throughout the world, of the order's mission. It seems fitting to include the prayer of St. Francis in these pages.

The Prayer of Saint Francis

Lord, make me an instrument of your peace,
Where there is hatred, let me sow love;
Where there is injury, pardon;
Where there is doubt, faith;
Where there is despair, hope;
Where there is darkness, light;
Where there is sadness, joy.
O Divine Master,

grant that I may not so much seek to be consoled, as to console;
to be understood, as to understand;
to be loved, as to love.
For it is in giving that we receive.
It is in pardoning that we are pardoned,
and it is in dying that we are born to Eternal Life.
Amen.

Maybe we are being called to live in greater harmony with each other's faiths. Perhaps we are being challenged to act as Mother Teresa did in her life–to believe in humanity when humanity doesn't always believe in itself.